Land Without Hats

Julie Mughal

Plain View Press
P. O. 42255
Austin, TX 78704

plainviewpress.net
sb@plainviewpress.net
1-512-441-2452

Copyright Julie Mughal, 2008. All rights reserved.
ISBN: 978-0-911051-41-4
Library of Congress Number: 2008934747

Cover art by Carla Caletti. For more information on her beautiful artwork, please visit: www.Carlacaletti.com

In loving memory of Pascal Baconnier

To the many courageous widows around the world whose stories remain untold
To my supportive and loving family and network of friends, both near and far
To my father who encouraged me long ago to write about my travels
To my husband, Imran, who has enthusiastically encouraged and supported me
and the project
To Sophia and Zachariah who help me to embrace life and love every day

Contents

Preface	7
Part I: Swissair 111	11
Part II: Widows' Journeys	25
The Cove	27
Dancing Spirits in the Northern Sky	31
In the Land Without Hats	37
The Boat of Sorrows	45
A Good Pair of Shoes to Make Your Way	57
Echoes Across the Sky	67
How Many Tears?	77
Don't Let Hope Slip	83
Part III: Forever Joined to the Sea and the Sky	93
Pakistani Moon	97
The Journey Continues...	98
Endnotes	99
About the Author	103

Preface

My first husband, Pascal, was killed when Swissair 111 crashed off the coast of Nova Scotia. At the age of thirty-two I found myself alone and widowed. As I struggled with this devastating loss, I sought meaning and a sense of purpose. At the time, I was working in Geneva, Switzerland for IOM – the International Organization for Migration – but found it too difficult to continue to live in Europe without Pascal. A little over a year after the accident, I moved back to the United States and settled in Connecticut, where my sister and her husband were living and began working at Save the Children.

One of the many saving graces of working for Save the Children was that, over time, I was not only able to slip back into a normal routine but also to lose myself in important work. I also found myself traveling frequently for my job. As a way to heal, I began to speak with widows from the many countries I visited. I owe an enormous debt to the many Save the Children colleagues in field offices around the world who helped to arrange interviews with local widows and who graciously agreed to translate from the myriad of local languages to English for me. What they translated were amazing stories of courage in the face of adversity. It opened up a world of widows that I never knew existed and inspired me to dig deeper into what it means to be a "widow" in different cultures.

In Haiti, I met three widows whom I've thought of many times in the years since I first began this journey of self-exploration and outreach. They lived in devastating poverty but their dignity belied this fact. They were strong and determined to continue to raise their children in circumstances few of us can imagine. Every day they struggled to make a living, keep their children in school, and deal with the shattering loneliness of managing these difficulties on their own.

They missed their husbands terribly but held onto the hope that they were now in a better place – *le pays sans chapeaux* – *the land without hats*. In this land, their husbands – hats in hand – met God for the first time and were welcomed into the kingdom of heaven. There they wait to be reunited with their loved ones one day.

In the years since Pascal's death, I've heard many widows voice this hope of a *land without hats* – as I have often done. The world to which their husbands have traveled is one of peace and has helped the women to continue their own journeys on earth.

Land without Hats is a collection of oral histories gathered from some of the places I visited since Pascal died. I've spoken with many exceptional women who continue their journeys – widows who have been faced with the struggle of re-creating their lives following the deaths of their husbands from causes ranging from landmine accidents in Afghanistan, to lack of medical facilities in Haiti, to squatter town violence in the Philippines. Often, the names of the widows and their family members have been changed out of respect for their privacy. When I've used the names of the widows and their families, I've received consent to do so.

Through their histories it becomes apparent that the plight of widows and the severity of the consequences of widowhood differ from one culture to another. Despite their many differences, there is one common thread that weaves through the stories of all the women – whether they are Pakistani, Bangladeshi, Haitian, or Nepalese – their overwhelming concern for the welfare of their children. Foremost in their thoughts and struggles is having enough food to properly nourish their children, money to pay for school fees, and the means to protect them against sexual abuse, violence, and exploitation.

It has been ten years since the accident that took Pascal's life. As the years passed – slowly at first, and more rapidly later – I've been able to do what many of us may take for granted – choose how to live the rest of my life. After the tragic events of September 11, 2001, I was sent to Save the Children's office in Pakistan to help with the unfolding humanitarian crisis. There I met, fell in love, and married Imran, a colleague who was working in the Islamabad office. In 2003, we moved to the United States and started a family. Sophia, our daughter, was born in September of that year and our son, Zachariah, was born two years later.

Unfortunately, there is not such a blessed and happy outcome awaiting many widows in the developing world who are bound by cultural, religious and societal norms from fully taking charge of their lives. Through no fault of their own, many are scorned and forced to live as outcasts in their societies.

In 2001, the Northwest Frontier Province of Pakistan was – and still is – a dangerous place. At the height of the Afghan refugee crisis, I met a widow outside a community health center waiting to have her ten-day-old newborn seen by a doctor. I never knew her name and she only agreed to speak with me in a concealed place, out of public view.

Her husband had been killed a few months earlier when he returned to Kunduz for a brief visit to check on the family's land. Kunduz, in northern Afghanistan, was the last major stronghold of the Taliban, who held power there until November 2001. During his brief return, a bomb struck the family's house and he was killed instantly, leaving behind three children and his pregnant wife.

I clearly remember the way her fearful eyes stared at me through the webbing of her pale blue *burqa*. Despite her covering, I could tell that she was very young. I remember seeing her eyes overflow with tears as she asked what kind of life her child would have, a widow's daughter.

To this day, this is one of the most haunting images I carry with me, mostly because I had no acceptable answer. It would be a life of hardship and struggle.

I am not an expert on widowhood, nor do I have training as a grief counselor. I was just a widow who listened to what other widows said about themselves, their families, and their lives both before and after their husbands died. I laughed and cried with the women and I wrote down what I heard. It's my hope that their histories will provide a glimpse into the lives of these widows – their struggles, heartaches, and triumphs. And that we might be able to find an answer to the question asked of me so many years ago – what kind of life will these women and their children lead? And, how can we make a difference?

Part I: Swissair 111

A *Swissair jet disappeared from radar screens Wednesday over the Atlantic Ocean near Nova Scotia, and there were unconfirmed reports that it may have crashed.*[1]

– CNN Breaking News, September 2, 1998, 11:16 p.m. (EST)

August 1998

My life is clearly delineated – life before Swissair 111 crashed into the Atlantic and life after. The last time I saw Pascal was in Manhattan on the corner of Forty-second and Lexington. It was a hot end-of-August day with an anticipation of the coming autumn in the air. Looking back, the summer of 1998 was a time of great promise and happiness. As we dodged the drippings from air conditioners far above our heads, the World Trade Center dominated the skyline at the tip of Manhattan Island. Pascal and I spent the morning together and met my sister for lunch.

As we walked downtown to Grand Central Station and across the street to the airport bus, I was overcome by sadness. I didn't want to return to Geneva without Pascal but I had to get back to my job and prepare for an upcoming trip to Guatemala. I was tempted to stay on an extra week but decided to return on my flight as planned.

I remember finally getting on the bus and settling myself in the seat. I held my hand against the air-condition-cooled window to reach out to him. The last image I have of Pascal is seeing him running alongside the bus waving good-bye.

Summer 1998

The summer of 1998 was an idyllic time for Pascal and me – a time of innocence. We seemed to live life with abandon and planned for a future that was full of promise.

Pascal and I were both in our early thirties and had been married for five years. We'd met in our twenties and were struck by what the French call a *coup de foudre* – a lightning bolt – roughly equivalent to the English "love at first sight." We were engaged within months of our first meeting and wed in New York in August 1993. We were inseparable. At the time, I was working for an international agency in Geneva, Switzerland, and Pascal was working just over the border in France. We were hoping to move to the United States and had been waiting for my transfer to Washington, D.C. During the spring of 1998, everything seemed to fall into place when news arrived that my transfer was finalized and we busied ourselves for the long-awaited move.

The months that followed were a time of great anticipation and excitement. Pascal had been hard at work studying for a degree in computer technology, hoping to break into the U.S. job market. While we had rarely been separated for longer than a week, Pascal decided to take computer classes in New York City. I would come to visit midway through his trip. That way we could spend our fifth wedding anniversary together and then fly back to Geneva together. It was all carefully planned.

That summer Pascal fell in love with New York. I could hear the excitement in his voice when we spoke over the phone. One of the many qualities I admired in Pascal was his sharp intellect as well as his innate curiosity and love of learning. He also was very determined and studied with an unwavering focus. He told me that the classes were going well, yet he still worried that he wouldn't pass his exams. I met Pascal as planned and we both stayed with my sister and brother-in-law in Connecticut. Pascal continued to commute into New York City to finish his classes and I busied myself preparing for my sister's upcoming wedding and our relocation to Washington.

Just before our scheduled return to Geneva, Pascal decided to stay an extra week in New York to allow him more time to prepare for his exams. I gathered up my courage and tried to make the best of it. I put aside my own disappointment of returning to Geneva alone, realizing that this was one of the moments in a marriage when you step aside for the other person, knowing that this extra time in New York was important to Pascal. I returned to our apartment in France and picked up my daily routine of commuting into Geneva for work.

On the night between September 2nd and 3rd, I went to bed thinking about Pascal's return the next morning. Pascal and I hadn't seen each other for about a week but it seemed much longer. I wasn't used to being alone in France without him and the week had been difficult waiting for his return.

I woke up abruptly one hour before the plane crashed. When I bolted up in bed, it took me a moment to sort out where I was and why I was alone. I had a terrible feeling that something was wrong. I tried to remain calm, reminding myself that I always let my imagination get the best of me, my mind quickly transforming a late arrival home into a car accident, a late phone call into bad news. The morning would come and, as planned, I would go pick up Pascal from the airport. He would come through the sliding doors at immigration, once he had picked up his luggage, and everything would be fine.

I turned on the news, thinking it silly to be so worried. About twenty minutes later, the "breaking news" headline appeared on the screen. I knew then, before the reporter came on to tell me and the world, that the plane had crashed and that my life would never be the same again. Ever.

September 2, 1998

Swissair 111 took off from New York's JFK airport at 8:18 p.m. on the evening of September 2, 1998. At 10:31 it crashed into the Atlantic Ocean off the Canadian coast – all 229 people aboard were killed.

At 4:00 in the morning – as the rest of Europe slept around me – I found myself utterly alone and in shock. I felt weak and my legs seemed to give out from underneath me. I didn't know what to do with this news and I'm not sure how I passed the many hours before friends suddenly began to appear at my door. I remember calling my family, who must have been equally in shock and desperate to be by my side.

The day after Pascal died was a beautiful September morning. The view of the mountains was stunning: the Alps and the Jura formed a crisp outline against the horizon as if a child had taken three crayons, one green for the Jura, one white for the Alps, and one a deep magenta for the sky.

Late in the afternoon I left my apartment to take a walk – as Pascal and I had done many times. I couldn't quite understand how life could continue normally for the people around me – the mothers shopping with their children, the people sitting at the cafes reading newspapers. I walked as if in a dream, wanting desperately to wake and have everything normal again for me.

Just twenty-four hours later, Swissair flew the relatives of the crash victims to Halifax, touching down on the runway that Swissair 111 had urgently tried to reach. My mother, brother, sister, and brother-in-law came to meet me and Yvonne, my mother-in-law, and I searched for them longingly when I arrived at the meeting point in downtown Halifax. It was the first time I saw my family after the accident and I was thankful to be close to them. The days that followed are a blur – there were briefings by the search and recovery team and the Canadian officials, trips to the crash site, official explanations of what had gone wrong. My family stayed by my side day and night.

Snippets of the days that followed have come back to me in fits and starts. The way my brother helped guide me through the interview with the forensic experts to help them identify Pascal once his remains were found. My mother sitting next to me on the bus as we made our way to Peggy's Cove, the closest landfall to the accident and the warmth and relief I felt by having her by my side. To this day I am profoundly touched when I remember her turning to me, a mother clearly grief-stricken for her daughter, and saying how she would forever love Pascal because he had made me so happy.

During these days, my sister was my constant companion, reliving memories of Pascal with me. She and her husband had hosted him during his month in the United States and she helped me fill in the details of Pascal's last week.

I also remember the way in which the small communities around Peggy's Cove embraced us and our pain. Many of them had heard what sounded like an explosion on the night of the accident and had rushed to the water's edge to see if they could help. Fishermen took out their boats to search for survivors in the dark, early morning hours following the crash despite the personal risk. The ever-present Royal Canadian Mounted Police helped us through these difficult days, not only through their compassion as they helped to escort us to the accident site, but in their small acts of kindness – a steady arm to bolster us during difficult moments and an outstretched hand to keep us from falling on the treacherous, rocky terrain of Peggy's Cove.

Autumn 1998

After the trip to Peggy's Cove, I relived many times in my mind the accident and what Pascal's last day might have been like. My sister has tried to fill me in on some of the details – I know that he went into New York with her on the train and then met her for lunch before heading for the airport. I know that he sent her flowers to thank her for her hospitality and help during his stay in America. He also called my mom to thank her.

I've imagined the long line when he arrived to check in for the flight. It was early September and I'm sure there were many French and Swiss tourists heading back home after their vacations touring the United States. There were always the United Nations workers who took what was informally known as the Swissair "shuttle." We had all taken it many times as we flew between Geneva and New York.

Next I imagine Pascal waiting in the dimly lit airport, anticipating his flight back home and waiting for the boarding announcement and the relief to finally get on the plane and settle in for the eight-hour trip back to continental Europe. I think that he was seated in 34A, next to a young man and his wife from the Midwest. Did they talk to each other, exchanging pleasantries on the transatlantic flight? I will never know for sure.

I try not to imagine what happened next – the announcement from the pilot about a problem, the fear and chaos. I've tried to protect myself from the final half hour but it has crept into my consciousness many times. To this day, I push it away and try to convince myself that the crash was quick and that Pascal and the others didn't have time to realize what was happening. But, I know this is not true.

Uncertainty is one of the most difficult aspects of losing a loved one in a plane crash. For months after the accident, I checked and rechecked the SA 111 JFK-GVA flight manifest. From my apartment in Ferney Voltaire, France, where we lived, I would log onto the Internet and pray that his name would not appear this time on the list. Yet each time I checked it was always the same, and Pascal was always on the list. It was hard to accept.

It was also hard to know if he was dead or alive. I sought out grief counselors, clergy, and other concerned people who told me that this was natural, especially when someone dies so young, so unexpectedly, so violently. It was especially true in the case of Swissair 111. The plane crashed a long way off shore and the impact was catastrophic. It would take months to identify the remains.

For many months that followed, I did not see a future but struggled to survive each hour, day, and week. Everyone advised me to get back into a routine. I continued to get up and go to work each day but I found it difficult to concentrate. The sense of purpose and meaning seemed to have drained from my life and the work I once loved.

It did help, however, to keep my mind occupied. I knew that there was a dangerous box tightly closed deep in my mind, filled with memories and emotions that I needed to protect myself from opening. I imagined it looked like an old grandmother's trunk in a dusty corner of an attic. My emotions were too raw to open the box – to delve too deeply into the loss and its enormity. The lost promise of a future with Pascal was too painful to accept and the memories of our happy past were too heartbreaking to allow myself to remember.

The accident continued to haunt me and the family and friends of the victims in more ways than one may imagine. The crash did not have the finality of other accidents. There was no complete "closure" for many months.

Despite the heroic and extraordinary efforts of the Canadian search teams, it took many months to receive notification that the remains of loved ones had been recovered. The distance from the shore and the depth of the wreckage – 180 feet below the surface – coupled with the turbulent Atlantic made for a difficult and often dangerous recovery effort.

It was a harrowing time, always waiting for the fateful but expected phone call to inform that remains had been recovered, which would end the wondering and put a certain finality to the death. All the next of kin had received provisional death certificates some days after the accident – issued out of respect but not exactly "by the book." This enabled many of the families to make arrangements concerning memorial services and wills. But it did not bring the finality that the call from the Royal Canadian Mounted Police would. My call arrived at the end of October, almost two months after the accident. This, again, was preliminary, as the recovery for remains continued well into the winter of 1999.

As December approached, I dreaded the thought of the upcoming holidays and Christmas. To allay my grief, my brother, Matthew, and I planned a trip to Nova Scotia for the day after Christmas. I longed to return to Nova Scotia to be close to Pascal. We landed in Halifax on a cold and snowy afternoon and it continued to snow heavily as darkness fell early over this small, cosmopolitan harbor. In contrast, the next morning was magnificent – a crisp, clear day – when we headed off on the coastal road to visit the closest land to the accident.

When we arrived at the small fishing village, the rocks leading up to the lighthouse and land's end were treacherous and slippery. On that bitter cold day in December, I looked out onto the restless Atlantic and felt closer to Pascal than I had in the months since his death. As I stood on the rocky coastline in the cold winds of the northern winter, I knew the road ahead would be difficult but I had a first glimmer that I would survive and could start to build a new life.

On that day ten years ago, the journey truly began. I placed a wreath of fresh evergreen clippings at a makeshift memorial nestled in the rocks. This was long before the Swissair 111 memorials were erected at Whalesback and Bayswater to honor those who died as well as the Nova Scotia coastal residents who heroically searched for survivors and then welcomed the victims' loved ones with such compassion.

As I looked out over the waves, I knew that Pascal would give me the strength to once again embrace life – to feel strong emotions and to enjoy beauty. I secured the wreath and whispered a prayer into the wind.

Winter and Spring

Throughout that long winter of waiting and uncertainty, there were also the many telephone calls alerting me and others who lost loved ones on the flight, that there was a new batch of "photo books" to look through. These were photographs, meticulously catalogued, of the thousands of belongings that had been recovered from the ocean floor. I wanted desperately to recover Pascal's wedding ring, but this was not to be. Like sea glass – the fabled "mermaids' tears" – it remains in the possession of the ocean until one day when it washes up somewhere on shore, still inscribed with his name and our wedding date, August 21, 1993.

I dreaded turning each unbearable page – and there were hundreds of them. My heart broke with every photo of a child's toy, a souvenir purchased on summer holiday, the jewelry that meant so much to the owner, a worn photograph with smiling faces.

On one of these terrible visits to New York City to look through the catalogue, I spotted Pascal's watch, which I had given him as a surprise birthday present. I both looked forward to and dreaded the package's arrival. It took me a long time to open the box and, once opened, I quickly resealed the package but the sight and smell of the watch – rusty and destroyed – remain with me to this day.

As Spring approached, I was finally notified that the recovery operations were completed and that Pascal could be put to rest. I couldn't bear the thought of Pascal making his final trip back to the United States unaccompanied. So I made what was to be a most harrowing journey to Canada with my sister and brother-in-law, to bring Pascal's body back to the United States. The mere notion of the trip overwhelmed me, but as I had many times since Pascal died, I summoned inner strength that I never knew existed. In my mind, I broke the trip down into manageable segments – departure from the United States, arrival in Halifax, appointment at the funeral parlor, departure from Canada.

During the same trip, I visited the hangar where the reconstruction of the airplane was taking place. To see the utter destruction of the aircraft brought finality to the tragedy. Where once there was hope that there had been survivors, there was now the acknowledgment that no one could have survived the impact.

As I waited for my flight back to Newark to be announced, I thought of Pascal's coffin on the tarmac, waiting to be loaded onto the plane. During the flight, it was both agonizing and comforting to know that Pascal was with me. I wanted to scream out to the other passengers that my husband had died and that his coffin was on board. Instead, I stared blankly out the window as the clouds sped by.

When I arrived at Newark, it seemed surreal for me to carry on with the trip home while Pascal's body was sent separately to the funeral home. I remember staring out at the runway, emotionally drained, not wanting to leave him behind, but knowing that the arrangements with the funeral home had been carefully put in place. The journey was not yet over and I braced for what I knew would be the most difficult days of my life.

A day later, I sat with Pascal's body at the funeral home. His coffin, beautiful and sterile, was neatly arranged with flowers. I stayed for a long time by his side, with my hand on the sleek wood. Overcome with grief and emotion, the tears, which had been pent up for months, finally flowed fiercely and freely, and I said my final goodbye.

The days that followed are a blur. My relatives and friends gathered at the cemetery in my hometown in upstate New York as prayers were said and flowers were placed on the casket as Pascal was lowered into the ground. It was as if I was playing the widow in a movie for which I hadn't rehearsed. After everyone had returned to their cars, I stood by the grave – just Pascal and me, for the last time. I left comforted that my father, buried a few headstones away, would keep Pascal company.

The Years That Followed

My family was my lifeline during these difficult days; we had all lived through loss before. My father died in 1987 when I was twenty-one years old. My mother was left a widow in her fifties. While you always know that your parents will not live forever, you are never prepared to accept it when it happens.

My older brother, younger sister, and I were young adults and had all moved out of the house – all living in upstate New York. My brother, four years my senior, had graduated and was living in Rochester; I was a senior at Syracuse University; and my sister, two years my junior, was also an undergrad at a university close by. My father had been sick for some time, but, to us, it was unimaginable that he would die – although I think we all knew deep down that his condition was terminal.

I remember receiving the phone call from my mother the week before Thanksgiving in my college dorm room. It was snowing out – it always seemed to be snowing in Syracuse. At first, she told me that we all needed to come home, that an ambulance had come to take my father to the hospital. I knew from her voice that it was more serious and she finally admitted that my father had passed away. My brother was already en route to pick me up and then we both wound our way through the Adirondacks on the cold autumn day to pick up my sister and go home.

It was a difficult time for all of us but my family's strong ties, encouraged and nurtured by my parents, saw us through. My mother kept life as normal as possible for us and, with her encouragement, we all went back to our upstate lives. I graduated a month later and came back home to live with my mother and grandmother. While my mother was devastated, her strong faith and love of her family kept her moving forward. She continued to work as an elementary school teacher, to run the house and to support us emotionally. I learned a great deal during that time about strength in the face of adversity – a role model that I would look to a decade later.

Indeed, the model served me well as I tried to find my way out of the dark tunnel that surrounded me. In the years following Pascal's death, my life moved in fits and starts – long nights of desperately searching the house for something, anything, that Pascal had left behind for me – a final note, an unwrapped present, a sign. There was also the restless wandering, back and forth between New York and Geneva and to the places where my job took me – Guatemala

City, Manila, Ho Chi Minh City– anywhere I could go to escape. Yet, somehow, my life continued.

I felt like I was drowning with sporadic attempts to surface for air. When I did, I frantically tried to put my life back together before being dragged down again. It was somewhere between Nairobi and Haiti that I "surfaced" and decided to speak with other widows. This was my project, which would carry me into the future. It allowed me to listen to other women tell their stories about surviving the terrible ordeal of widowhood.

It was a way of healing myself, while also trying to help others.

Part II: Widows' Journeys

Footfalls echo in the memory
Down the passage we did not take
    Toward the door we never opened.[2]

–T.S. Eliot

The Cove

Many have seen the Cove in sunlit noon,
  So few have gazed in graying haze…shifting
    scenes in rolling mist…[3]
                    – William deGarthe

What is it like for me to return to the place where my husband was killed? To go back to Nova Scotia – a beautiful, wild spot – and realize that part of me died when Swissair 111 crashed into the Atlantic on the evening of September 2, 1998? I've made the journey many times. I believe that it was only there that I could start again – it was only in confronting the loss that I could truly move forward.

There's something about the beauty of the place and the kindness of its people that brings me great comfort. It has been instrumental in my healing process. I felt that I was not alone on this island that was no stranger to tragedy. Among the many accidents and shipwrecks that have occurred off its coast, the most famous is the Titanic. Over two hundred of its victims are interred in Halifax, the provincial capital of Nova Scotia.

Its beauty belies the tragedies it conceals. The winter is stark and dramatic, the autumn is a breathtaking explosion of deep and bright colors, and the long-awaited spring is a true awakening of life. But the summer is absolutely magnificent.

My sister, Becky, and I met Agnes one month shy of the second anniversary of the accident. Agnes is the widow of one of Nova Scotia's most famous artists, William deGarthe, and a formidable force in her own right. When we met her, she was the curator of the William deGarthe Gallery in Peggy's Cove, the keeper of his legacy and an unofficial ambassador for people visiting this remote coastal village. She will never know how many times in the intervening years I've thought of her and our brief meeting.

On the night Swissair crashed, Agnes went to bed early in her small village of fifty residents, not realizing what the night would bring and the terrible tragedy that would unfold so close to her home.

She was awakened early on the morning of September 3rd by a telephone call. Upon hearing the news, she quickly looked out her window to see St. Margaret's Bay ablaze with emergency vehicles – recovery efforts were already well underway.

In contrast, the day Becky and I visited, Peggy's Cove had again returned to a small coastal community in the final days of a glorious summer. When we entered the William deGarthe Gallery, the late afternoon sun was streaming through a large bay window overlooking the Atlantic. Agnes didn't see us at first; she was seated quietly contemplating the ocean and the rocks of this tiny fishing village perched precariously on one of the last footholds of North America. We could see her seated in profile – an elderly woman, brightly dressed in a green suit.

When she turned to greet us, Agnes playfully asked us to guess her age. It was impossible for us to know that she was ninety-four, born in 1906 when the last century was still young. She had seen so much, this was obvious in her lively eyes and her knowing smile. One could only imagine the exciting life she had led with her husband, William deGarthe, who had been a famous sculptor and painter in his adopted homeland of Canada.

When she looked up, I was struck by her sharp blue eyes, which sparkled and danced when she spoke. She told us that William had traveled from Finland in 1926 to Canada at the age of nineteen. Once married, he told his bride that she had to see Peggy's Cove, a beautiful fishing village, which he sometimes referred to as the "pearl of the Atlantic."[4] Some say the cove is named after Peggy, a mythical woman washed up by the sea. Agnes and William visited. "And," Agnes said quite matter-of-factly, "we stayed."

Willliam and Agnes spent their summers in Peggy's Cove and in 1955 moved to the village. For half a century, deGarthe painted the sea and the land and the critical juncture where they become one.

He painted and carved ordinary fishermen and sloops and the heroic Peggy of legend.

Agnes told us that her husband had died seventeen years ago. According to his wish, he was buried in the granite walls of the *Fishermen's Monument*, which he began carving at the age of seventy. Today, it stands sentinel near the entrance to Peggy's Cove and is a reminder of deGarthe's great respect for the sea and his love of his adopted home.

Agnes knowingly smiled when I mentioned that her husband's work had brought me great comfort. I thought of the strikingly beautiful deGarthe mural behind the tiny altar of St. John's Church in Peggy's Cove, which shows Jesus with an outstretched hand leading a boat of distressed fisherman to safe shores.

As I left the gallery, Agnes looked out at the ocean. I could only imagine the memories that must be flashing through her mind – happy images of picnics with her husband from days long past, Agnes reading, William painting. A young couple, secure in their happiness, reveling in their youth and the promise it held.

I've visited the gallery many times since but have never seen Agnes again. However, I have a daily reminder of her playful energy and enthusiasm for life – and a bit of Peggy's Cove – when I look at the deGarthe painting, signed by Agnes, that hangs over my mantle in Connecticut. Its gentle colors and fishing boats muted by the morning haze remind me of this small community, which has become – unintentionally but indelibly – a part of my life's story.

Dancing Spirits in the Northern Sky

> *Long he walked down his path. Ahead of him was a row*
> * of lights, close to the horizon.*
> *That he knew, was his destination, jiibayag niimi'idiwag,*
> * the northern lights...There they danced and feasted.*[5]
> *   – Winona LaDuke, Last Standing Woman*

In the Ojibwe language, July is *aabitaniibinogiizis*, the "month of the midsummer moon." I traveled to the border of North Dakota and Minnesota during the midsummer moon to visit an English language camp for children where I'd established a scholarship program in Pascal's memory. The director of the school kindly made some phone calls before my arrival and arranged for me to meet with Marilyn, who lived on the White Earth Reservation.

I always like to explore new places. Despite being tired from the flight halfway across the country, I was excited to walk around a scorching Fargo. Downtown Fargo retains the ruggedness of a western town founded in 1871 and the charm of a place that has not yet fully succumbed to modernization. A freight train runs through the city and you can hear its lonely whistle in the evenings as it makes its way across the vast stretches of continent.

Later, as I settled into my hotel and rested from my flight, I thought of the many small towns, similar to Fargo, which Pascal and I had explored during our extended trips "out West." I let my mind wander back to our summer "home leaves" from Geneva when we would drive, not knowing exactly where the long, straight roads and open spaces would take us.

Living in France, America became a mythical place – especially the West with its spectacular landscapes and natural beauty. Growing up, I'd never left the East Coast, so Pascal and I explored the West together. In a very immediate sense, we went in search of America – the America in which we planned to settle down, raise our family, and grow old together.

The next day, I made the three-hour trek north and east to Bemidji, through the green flatness of Minnesota which, during the drive, slowly gave way to rolling hills and forests. Along the way, I saw bald eagles soaring in a magenta-blue sky over small towns and vast stretches of forest. As I traveled on the straight, hot highway, mirages of wet expanses of road would suddenly appear on the horizon and playfully disappear. I could never quite catch up with their evasive images as they escaped into the wide-open spaces.

Bemidji is beautiful in an untouched way. One cannot help but wonder what it was like when the land was still called *Gaawaawaabiganikaag*, or White Earth, by the original inhabitants. As far back as history can be recalled in this remote corner of North America, at the source of the mighty Mississippi, there were the Anishinabe, the "first people." Their neighbors referred to them as "the peoples who make pictographs" or "Ojibwe."[6] It was through pictographs, symbols, and stories that they told their history.

Embedded in their sad story, one would hear the *dibaajimokwe*, storyteller, recount how waves of peoples came to settle this beautiful White Earth and how the Ojibwe began a long struggle to retain their rich culture and history.

After spending the morning in Bemidji, visiting the language camp where I'd established the scholarship fund in Pascal's memory, I raced to Mahnomen, some forty-five minutes south on Highway 59 to meet with Marilyn, a recently widowed Native American. I missed her by minutes but did get the chance to speak with her a few weeks later from my home in Connecticut.

Marilyn was fifty-six when we spoke. Her husband, Charles, died one month before their thirty-fifth wedding anniversary – just six weeks after he'd been diagnosed with bone cancer. Marilyn confided with difficulty that she was glad the end came quickly. "Bone cancer is very painful," she explained. Charles was Ojibwe; Marilyn is from a mixed heritage – her mother was Ojibwe, her father was French and Swedish.

Marilyn was born in the Nay-tah-waush area of the reservation. Her father was a road construction foreman, which meant that she spent much of her childhood away from the reservation, traveling in Montana and Wyoming. Her father would choose neighbors to work on the road crews with him and they would all travel together to different work sites. She added fondly, "I had a good childhood. I was very lucky."

Marilyn, being born into a "mixed family," did not learn Ojibwe. Her grandparents spoke their native language but by the time her mother was born, it was "frowned upon" for her to speak it. Indeed, Marilyn's mother was sent to one of the many boarding schools forced upon Native American children.

This practice, which began in 1869 under President Ulysses S. Grant, continued well into the twentieth century as part of the federal government's assimilation policy and has left indelible emotional scars to this day. Marilyn told me that her mother joined "a whole group of children with no one to look after them" in a place where they were not allowed to speak their language or learn their traditions. All told, over one hundred thousand Native American children would be forced to attend these government-sanctioned schools and be raised Christian.[7]

Despite the long trips away for her father's work and her mother's difficult history, Marilyn always considered the White Earth Reservation her home. She and Charles, who was five years her senior, grew up in the same community and married when she turned eighteen. "We just met and started going out together," she told me, adding that her husband was well liked and had many friends.

While Marilyn was spending time off and on the reservation, her future husband was growing up in a more traditional Native American household. Charles's parents were Ojibwe and he danced at powwows as a child. His grandmother and aunt are famous Ojibwe basket makers and Marilyn proudly noted that their work is on display at the Smithsonian Museum.

Despite his more traditional upbringing, Charles grew up Episcopalian. Before he died, he requested that native customs not be integrated into his funeral ceremony – no *dewe'igan* or drum pounding, no plates of food brought to his grave, no traditional Ojibwe hymns. "Many people do not want to mix Christian and traditional Ojibwe rites," Marilyn explained.

The year following Charles' death, Marilyn's life fell apart. "I was not able to make good, sound decisions – I was not thinking correctly." She spent most of the first year "running away from things," at one point even quitting her job. Marilyn skipped family gatherings, despite being very close to her in-laws. She told me, "When they say you have a broken heart – well, you really do."

Marilyn finally stopped running, finding the support she needed in her family and her minister. "The people that surrounded me before my husband died are the same that embraced me after he died – they have not put me at a distance." When I spoke with Marilyn, she told me that her life was slowly coming together and that she felt more grounded. She had even found the courage to return to family gatherings for the holidays.

Marilyn visits her husband's grave a few times a year to honor his memory, admitting, however, that that she doesn't feel much emotion at his tombstone. She feels very strongly that he is not there, telling me that "he is in a much better place."

When Marilyn told me this, I thought of the Elizabeth E. Frye poem that I kept tucked in my wallet for many years following Pascal's death. *Do not stand on my grave and weep, I do not sleep./I am the thousand winds that blow, I am the diamond glints on snow.../Do not stand on my grave and cry; I am not there, I did not die...*[8] It became worn from being unfolded, read and carefully refolded back in its secret corner of my purse, helping me through many difficult moments. I never knew when I would need the comfort of reading it – excusing myself from dinner with friends to find a quiet place to reflect on it, unfolding it during ceaselessly long hours on transatlantic flights, sitting at coffee shops reading it amongst strangers.

Marilyn is confident that she will be reunited with Charles one day. Until that time, her mantra is: "Make yourself get up and get on with life."

When I spoke with her many years later, Marilyn had done just that. Today, she is an ordained Episcopalian minister and was grateful that her mother, who died at the age of eighty-eight, lived long enough to see her daughter reconnect with life. "We miss her greatly," Marilyn confided, "but it was a joy for me to be able to spend her final years of life with her. During this time I was also taking classes to become a minister. She lived long enough to see me ordained a deacon of the church."

Marilyn has found a meaningful path and an inner peace. She told me recently, "I find my life filled to overflowing with everything that I have to do." I was greatly inspired by Marilyn and her strength of character and purpose.

In reflecting upon my time in Northern Minnesota and Marilyn, my mind often returns to a very striking passage by Anne Dunn, an Ojibwe storyteller and writer from White Earth: *I've been told when we get to the end of our road, we will be asked three questions: Did you enjoy the journey? Were you kind to your relatives? The third question is a secret because it is just for you.* [9]

What will my third question be? What will Marilyn's be when she reaches the Northern Lights? What were the third questions reserved for our husbands? These are the secrets that each of us carries as our journey continues.

In the Land Without Hats

> *The women all told me that their husbands were safe in "the land without hats."*

There is an indescribable mystique about Haiti. It is a mesmerizing and troubled country. I arrived in Haiti in the summer of 2000, during a particularly difficult time of political upheaval. Yet the electricity and dynamic energy of the country and people were palpable.

Haiti was the first French-speaking country I visited after Pascal's death and I felt an immediate connection – it somehow felt familiar. As I slipped between English and French, the beautiful lilt of the Haitian Creole, the African/Caribbean sister language of French, transported me back to my early days in Geneva when I worked as the desk officer for Africa at an international organization.

In many ways, Haiti reminded me of my numerous trips to Africa – especially Malawi during the troubled Banda years – a terrible dictator who ruled the southern African country with an iron fist. After Pascal and I met, my first trip was to Malawi. Eight summers later, when I landed at the Toussaint Louverture International Airport in Haiti, I remembered thinking that Pascal would not be happy to know I was again going to such a difficult, often violent place.

I frequently needed to remind myself that I was in the Caribbean and not in sub-Saharan Africa. There were many similarities: the lush landscape, dusty towns, devastating poverty and a people who emanated warmth despite the hardships they faced. Yet Haiti was geographically a world away. Just six hundred miles from America's coast, it has some of the worst development indicators in the Western hemisphere.

Upon awaking in a foreign land, I'm always struck by the unique sounds of a country as it faces a new day. As the first tentative rays of light streaked across the sky, I remember hearing the Creole roosters sing their insistent *kokioko* – their own form of the English *cock-a-doodle-doo* – while the equally persistent songs of the cicadas signaled the end of a warm, balmy night fanned by the northeast trade winds. I could hear the bells of vendors and street merchants readying for business in the steep and crevice-ridden streets of Port-au-Prince. There is a comfort to know that the world outside is awakening – before the heat of the day releases its full fury on the land.

In contrast, the sounds of the Haitian night are few. The lives of villagers in remote areas of the world are often steeped in ancient traditions and entrenched in folklore. In Haiti, the dark provides a portal into this world. Under the cover of darkness, an evil has gripped Haiti from century-old tales of werewolves – the *loups garou* – to the more recent Tonton Macoutes of the Duvalier years and their brutality.

I soon left the capital, Port-au-Prince, on a small plane headed north to Maïssade. It quickly became obvious why the Taino, the original inhabitants of *Ayti*, or Haiti, had referred to their island as the "mountainous land." The Taino lived in Ayti long before Columbus landed there in early December 1492, "discovering" the new world and losing one of his famous ships, the Santa Maria, as it sank in its waters. Under subsequent generations of Europeans, the Taino saw their land become the colony of Saint Dominique and, upon independence from France in 1804, it again became Haiti, the land of mountains.[10] Maïssade is a village tucked away behind these mountains, which lead to Port-au-Prince. It's a lush and remote region with mango trees that struggle under the weight of their juicy, sweet load.

This *plateau centrale* is a poor land inhabited by a population, old before its time, who struggle to survive in this economically deprived land. Maïssade is also a region with many children, stunted by malnutrition and hungry for education.

As I walked through the dusty market of Maïssade, I took in the sights and smells of the bustling *marché* in the final moments before closing. The adults and children alike were curious – I must have been one of the few foreign visitors to their isolated part of the world. The adults smiled and offered a tentative *bonsoir*, the same in French as in Creole, while the more adventurous of the children spoke with me, came close, and touched my hair. The vendors were all eager to sell one last cup of beans, one last stalk of sugar cane as the flies eagerly awaited to attack what remained as the merchants began to rise from their mats and pack up for the day.

Before sunset, I traveled to the even more remote hamlet of Dos Bois Pins where the young children, especially the girls with beautiful rows of braids decorated with the brightest of bows, sang for us in French: *envoler papillions*, fly away butterflies.

Early the next morning, I was awakened by the sound of banging drums, leading the villagers to prayer. When I emerged from the small guesthouse, the rutted roads were already busy and crowded. What struck me most were the many beautiful, dignified women, brightly dressed and heavily burdened with baskets balanced firmly on their heads. They competently navigated the roads, still rutted and pooled with water from recent flooding. Without missing a step, they would warmly greet me and indicate the best pathway to follow without getting wet, "Take the small path in the bushes that leads up and away from the deep puddle."

Haitian women are strong and capable and this was confirmed by the three women who met me in Maïssade to share their stories. (*The names in this chapter have been changed.*) The Save the Children office had arranged for me to meet with Camille, Manette, and Francine, three widows who lived in the area where our programs were being implemented. Despite their obvious poverty, they came dressed in their best outfits. At first, they were hesitant to speak but soon felt comfortable once they heard my own story of becoming a widow. Despite having lived different lives, there was a thread that wove our destinies together, an unspoken complicity that I've noticed many times in many different places throughout the world.

For over an hour, the three women bravely let me glimpse into their world and for a brief moment, I could begin to comprehend the challenging lives they lead as widows in a remote, poor, and troubled land.

I spoke through a translator, asking the questions in English and then strained to understand the bits of French embedded in their Creole answers. Camille took the lead. She had been widowed the longest – some eleven years. She told us that she was forty-two, although she looked much older. She well might have been – birth and death records can be quite sketchy and imprecise, even nonexistent, in remote, outlying provinces in Haiti and elsewhere around the world.

Camille spoke with conviction in a straightforward manner. She bore her suffering nobly and it was obvious she had suffered greatly. Yet, her story hinted at a softer, more animated person who had been buried with her husband.

Camille met Gilles – *un ami dans le quartier*; "a friend from the neighborhood" – as a young teenager. They attended the same school, fell in love, and had their first child when she was fifteen. Camille and Gilles had been together for over a decade when he passed away, leaving the thirty-one-year-old to raise five children – three girls and two boys. One of Camille's regrets is that they never married. However, she explained that it would have cost too much to obtain the birth certificates and the marriage license as well as pay for the ceremony and the reception. Camille's husband is buried in Maïssade.

Manette, dressed in black, was seated next to Camille. Her husband had died just two months before the interview. She was still in shock and it was a great tribute to her inner strength that she had agreed to speak with me. She was obviously still weakened from the overwhelming sorrow of a very traumatic loss and the strain showed clearly on her face.

Camille, who sat by her side, felt the rawness of the loss and stroked Manette's arm to comfort her. She began by telling us that her husband, Emile, died suddenly while at work in the family's field. Manette received a message that her husband had fallen ill. By the time she arrived, he had already passed away. Emile left behind *dix enfants* – the same in French as in Creole – ten children: four girls and six boys ranging in age from young adult to a fifteen-month-old baby. Manette had also known her husband since childhood and told us that they had their first child when she was about fifteen years old.

The last woman to speak was Francine; she was the youngest member of the group – looking much younger than her thirty-seven years. A woman or girl in mourning in Haiti wears black not just for a husband, but also when her father, mother, or sibling dies. Francine came dressed in black for her recently deceased father. She told me that if a woman could afford mourning attire – the black outfit is handmade and expensive – then it is customary to wear it for two years.

Despite her recent loss, Francine smiled often and her inner beauty shone through, especially during the animated moments when she spoke of her courtship. She smiled shyly, recounting that she and Bernard had dated for just six month before marrying. She laughed, saying, "It didn't take a long time!" Everyone smiled at this – especially me. It had been the same for Pascal and me – we were engaged just four months after meeting and married a little over a year later. I thought they must have been a handsome couple.

Francine's happy memory soon faded as she told us of Bernard's illness and death. "He suffered greatly before he died," she told us and explained that he had been sick for a long time and she'd spent all her money trying to find a cure. Despite these efforts, he succumbed to his illness – a young man with a young family. After nine years of marriage, Francine was left to raise three children. Francine was widowed at thirty-three, just one year older than I had been.

There is a deep faith in Haiti – with a majority of the residents following Catholicism. Camille and Francine are Catholics; Manette, Baptist. All three had clearly been bolstered by their religious devotion that had helped them through their most difficult times. After losing their husbands and during the first difficult months of adjustment, the women told me that their communities and *lakou*, extended family, helped in preparing food, taking care of their children, and came "just to keep us company" during the loneliest hours.

"Women from the community came to visit," said Manette, "and just sat and talked and tried to give me encouragement. They spent time with me so that I would not feel alone." For Camille, it was the local church group that came to her house. "They came and gave me comfort," she said. "The group chose prayers and called on the Trinity to give me strength."

Their families and the communities provided the widows with what they could; but they have all suffered financial hardship. The three women, all acquaintances before our meeting, said their husbands had worked the fields for a living. Small plots are valuable commodities – a lifeline to raise food and fresh produce, which the women sell at the market. The scant living they make from these small stalls at the local outdoor *marché* is used to send their children to school and to ensure that their families stay healthy.

The land owned by Manette and Emile had provided for their ten children. It was the land that Emile went to till and harvest long hours every day, the same field where he died, and the land that was sold to pay for his funeral. Manette, still in shock after only two months of widowhood, calmly recounted that she had no land left and did not own her own home. She and her children now live off the charity of her family. Camille also sold her family's land to pay for her husband's burial expenses – which surely included the *mange morte*, the traditional "meal of the dead" offered to mourners after a funeral.

Francine did not mention land but said that her husband's family gave her and her three children a place to live. "My husband's family does not want me to leave with the children," she explained. They have a roof over their heads, but since her husband died, she can no longer afford to send her children to school. There was desperation in her voice and her expression seemed to ask, "What type of future will they face?"

At a time of questioning, such as this, the women take needed strength from their belief that their husbands are safe with the Lord in *le pays sans chapeaux* – the land without hats – an expression for heaven. I encountered many such examples of steadfast faith among widows during my conversations with them throughout the world.

Francine, with a faraway look, expressed her unwavering belief that she would be with Bernard again. She was comforted to know that he is in the "Lord's hands," and added confidently, "My husband was not into bad things." Camille seemed a bit less sure of the mysteries of life after death but she also concurred that she would see Gilles again "in spirit" because he had been a good man. She quickly added, "I hope I will" – expressing that nagging bit of doubt that widows usually suppress – too terrible to be spoken. Lifting our spirits, Manette confidently told us that her husband was in contact with the Lord adding, "I'm sure that I'll find him again one day. I'd like that."

Francine, Camille, and Manette all agreed that their futures are in the hands of the Lord. While Haitian widows can remarry after a two-year waiting period, it was quietly added that many men would not want to take on the responsibility of a widow and her children.

There is a folktale in the Haitian oral tradition that warns a man of the responsibility he takes on when he marries into such a union. In the *Singing Bone Story*, men are told: "Choose whom you want to marry, but if you choose a tree that has fruit, you must care for the fruit as much as for the tree."[11] Many men, the women told me, find the burden recounted in this fable, too heavy to take on.

Camille's advice to newly widowed women such as Manette is to "live the way I and the others present are living. Don't put your children through misery." She further added, "Whenever a man has a child with a woman, the woman needs to provide and take care of them." Francine added, "Fight and work hard for your children, do not leave them behind."

The three women, who had been so kind and patient in speaking with me, added one final piece of advice, breaking out in laughter at the Creole expression they pronounced, "*Tout koukou klere pou je'w*" – "all cuckoo birds shine in your eyes," or everyone needs to take care of herself – and added, "Move forward." "*Degaje'w.*" This very pragmatic piece of advice – one which I vowed to live – nicely summed up the resilience and strength of these three extraordinary women.

The Boat of Sorrows

> *From the sea of gladness, a flood poured out today... Take up your oars, sit down, row merrily. No matter how heavy the load is we'll get the boat of sorrow to the other shore.*[12]
>
> – Rabindranath Tagore, *Gitanjali*

In a Bangladeshi folktale it is written, "Fifteen nights of moonlight are followed by fifteen nights of darkness. After happiness there is always sorrow."[13] In Hindu and Muslim cultures, white is often associated with mourning. This is in great contrast to the Indian subcontinent's burst of colors that enliven your senses at every turn.

I arrived in Bangladesh in September 2000, just two years after Pascal's death. The smells, noises and colors – beautiful colors – of this densely populated country enlivened my senses. Feeling a bit overwhelmed, I remember traveling through Dhaka, the country's bustling capital, and promising myself that I would just sit back and enjoy the sights of the city and its people – knowing full well that years later, images of Bangladesh and its dynamic energy would come to mind, random snippets of a faraway place serving as a bridge to the person I've become. The cacophony of sounds and sights continued as the rickshaws wove their intricate patterns through the traffic in a whirl of pinks, blues, and greens.

I left Dhaka almost immediately after arriving to begin the five-hour trek to Nasirnagar where I met a widow from the community. Nasirnagar is a district in the northeast corner of Bangladesh, brushed up against neighboring India. During the long and bumpy journey, I was struck first by the number of people – at that time there were about 120 million Bangladeshis or some 2,200 people per square mile.[14] People were ever present, as was water – both a blessing and a curse. Bangladesh is situated at the confluence of two great rivers: the Ganges from the east and the Brahmaputra from the north, and some seven hundred others, each winding its way through this flat, often flooded country.

Water and people – the ferry landings were crowded as we waited to cross the many rivers and deltas on our way north. Men would gather around us in their traditional *lungi* sarongs and the women and girls in their beautiful *saris*. They would often stare, not quite daring to approach us, curious as to who we were and where we were going. As always, the children would gather closer, curious, not so inhibited by the constraints of their society. Our last crossing into the Nasirnagar region was by boat. The sun was setting, and as I sat on the large straw roof, wondering what lay ahead, the most spectacular sunset unfolded before my eyes, a large red illumination above the flooded delta.

At daybreak, I woke to see more clearly that the guesthouse where I had slept was situated on a small lake. Despite the early hour, women and girls had already begun to gather on the lake's edge to wash clothes, bathe their children, and gather water for the day. The long hours worked by women in the developing world have always struck me with each passing voyage. The day of a woman on the Asian subcontinent is no different, often beginning in the early hours of the morning and not finishing until long after the evening meal.

The first woman I encountered in Nasirnagar was Amina, a widow who assisted at the guesthouse. At the time of his death, her husband had three wives; Amina was the third. She looked old, but I'm sure she wasn't. Women in remote areas of Bangladesh often look much older than their years – especially the widowed, who are among the most destitute and vulnerable subgroup of the society. Amina had been lucky to find employment and was always close at hand, shyly greeting us with her traditional *pranaam*, bowed head and joined palms; eagerly pouring us cups of sugary, delicious tea. Despite the language barrier, I felt a warmth that emanated from her. Perhaps it was particularly directed at me, a bond that needed no spoken words.

As the sun rose higher in the white-hot sky, colorfully patterned and decorated rickshaws awaited me as I descended into the bright day. Again, the path to the neighboring village was not direct, but wove its way across rivers and flooded plains. During the days in Nasirnagar, I visited many villages but the last, for me, was the most memorable. In this particularly remote village, I met with a number of local women who, with Save the Children's guidance, had formed a savings group.

Like all other days during our visit, it was very hot as we joined a weekly meeting being held inside a tin-roofed hut. The temperature inside was almost unbearable but this did not deter the women from carrying out their business; when we entered, they were engaged in intense discussions.

About twenty entrepreneurial women were seated on the dirt floor with their legs tucked to the side. They offered me gestures of welcome; immediately someone was by my side with a fan. The fan, held agilely in the right hand, was twirled expertly around the wrist, giving off a much-welcomed breeze. The children, not allowed inside, approached as closely as they dared, curious to see what was happening in this adult world.

I met with the women and discussed their situations. The loans provided through a Save the Children program helped them to improve their lives, to finance projects that otherwise would remain unrealizable dreams. One woman told of how a loan had saved her youngest daughter from acute pneumonia – without it she would have been unable to seek out the urgent attention needed to save her.

Rasika, a member of the group, went unnoticed by me during the visit to the crowded hut, despite her telltale white *sari*. (*The names in this chapter have been changed.*) The absence of color is normally quite striking in such a colorful country. She must have been seated in the back, trying not to draw undue attention to herself. I thought that must be how Rasika conducted her life as a young Hindu widow in the outlying region of Nasirnagar – unnoticed, uncared for, invisible. Rasika was one of the few Hindus I met in Bangladesh, a country that is predominately Muslim. Later, she graciously sat down with me, two of her five children by her side, and recounted the story of her young life.

The first thing I noticed about Rasika was her frailty. She seemed to be truly alone. It was a difficult interview and she often looked pained, more so than many of the other women I had spoken with in other parts of the world.

When I visited Rasika, it was the lunar month of *Bhaadra*, which falls in August/September. It's a traditional time to honor Ganesha, the god known as the remover of obstacles. I reflected later that Rasika must often pray to the elephant-headed god and lord of beginnings. There were many obstacles in her life. Indeed, Rasika faced difficulties that many of us can only imagine in this, one of the poorest countries in the world.

Rasika evoked in me deep feelings of sympathy. When speaking with other widows, I often felt that despite their difficulties, they would be okay, they would manage. With Rasika, it was different. Her misfortune and the means available in her society to overcome the hardships appeared to be, in a certain sense, insurmountable. Her plight seemed desperate; her future, and that of her children, uncertain.

At sixteen, life was going as planned. Like most Hindus in this remote area, Rasika's parents arranged her marriage and she moved to her husband's village. The young newlyweds took up residence in the house of an uncle; a practice not unusual in this close-knit, family-oriented society. Indeed, often many generations of an extended family will live together in a *bari* or small hamlet of homes situated around a common courtyard.

Ten years later, things began to go terribly wrong. Rasika told me of her husband's death from a "high fever." Often, in rural pockets of South Asia, the cause of death is not more precise than that. Rasika told me he suffered for fifteen to twenty days and died, perhaps, she said, due to an allergic reaction to a medicine that he had taken. Her husband was twenty-eight at the time of his death and they had been married for ten years.

After her husband's death and the *shraddha*, or rituals associated with a life's passing, the community gathered at Rasika's house to express sympathy. However, their assistance soon dropped off and, after her husband was cremated, Rasika and her children continued to live with her husband's uncle, whose role, as the eldest surviving male in the paternal line, had become one of protector of his brother's family.

Rasika bravely described the days following her husband's death: "I ate only plain rice, without sauce or vegetables, and drank liquids for fifteen days." Rasika told me that every day she prepared her portion of rice, put it outside the house, and waited for the black crow to arrive. "If the crow ate the rice, I would also be allowed to eat rice on that day." This ritual continued for fifteen days following the cremation ceremony – harkening back to the fifteen days of darkness in the folktale. Later, I also found in the folklore of the subcontinent a reference to *bali kakka*, or crows, which the deceased send to eat the food left for them by friends and relatives.

As Rasika told her story, her youngest daughter began to squirm in her lap and cry. Rasika reached for her breast to feed the baby, who was dressed in a bright pink smock, as her sister looked on. Both children had very short hair and Rasika's eldest daughter wore hoop earrings and a bright stud in her pierced nose – the traditional signs of feminine adornment. This contrasted sharply with her mother's soiled white dress and lack of any jewelry. Indeed, one of the rituals that Rasika was surely subjected to was the smashing of her glass bangles – which are proudly worn by married women – to signal the beginning of widowhood.

Holding back her tears as she breastfed her baby, Rasika expressed her firm belief that her husband had gone to a better existence despite the belief by some villagers that he had been reincarnated as a spirit. If they were correct, this would mean that Rasika's husband still struggled through his journey of birth and rebirth – not yet at his final destination.

In many cultures, the widow is blamed for her husband's death and she can become a symbol of bad luck. Rasika felt that her status in the small community had been inalterably changed. "The villagers do not accept me gladly, I am treated differently," she noted on the verge of tears. "During my husband's lifetime, he was my social link to the community." She worked as a maid at the time her husband died but could no longer find work. When I met her, Rasika was raising ducks and selling them in the market as her sole source of income. She found it difficult to feed her children, to dress them, and to ensure that they attended school – the type of difficulties, Rasika said, that she would never have encountered if her husband were still alive.

Rasika told me that she wouldn't remarry, noting forcefully, "I'm not interested." Later, during discussions with a village doctor and other women in the community, I was told that it would be virtually impossible for Rasika to find a new husband because of her status as a widowed mother.

Rasika often spoke of her hardships with her brother, sister, and relatives who lived some two kilometers away in the neighboring village. However, the most important advice she received came from other women in the community. They told her that she must become economically self-sufficient – an enormous challenge for any woman in rural Bangladesh, but most especially for a widow raising five children.

Rasika, however, was trying, despite the difficulties she faced. She joined the women's savings group and participated with them in income-generating activities. That helped to supplement her income. She hoped it would allow her to send her small children to school and to protect them from the hardships they would encounter – to break the cycle of poverty that they were subjected to after her husband's death.

There is a beautiful poem in the *Gitanjali* penned by the Bengali poet Rabindranath Tagore in the early twentieth century: *From there the sun and stars take their streams of light in golden vessels, and so unending life is scattered throughout the sky.*[15] I think of this beautiful verse when I remember Pascal – and when my thoughts harken back to Rasika. I wonder, when Rasika looks into the star-filled sky of Nasirnagar once the rainy season has come to its tumultuous end, what she sees…

And, what does Sabina see when she looks into that same night sky some one hundred miles away in Dhaka, the capital of Bangladesh?

Dhaka was founded in the seventeenth century but cities have stood on its foundations for over a thousand years. It has a rich history, ruled by the Moguls and later the British when East Bengal formed part of the famed precious jewels in the British Raj's crown until 1947.

The partition of the sub-continent in 1947 created the new nation of Pakistan which, in reality, created two Pakistans – one to the west and the other 1,000 miles to the east. Some twenty-five years later, "East Pakistan" declared independence and out of the crucible of conflict, modern-day Bangladesh was born in 1971.[16]

In 1971, Sabina was a bright student in Dinajpur, well on her way to completing secondary school. Sabina very graciously agreed to meet me one evening, after a long day of work at a national training and rehabilitation center for destitute women – a job she'd held since her husband's death in 1997.

As she entered Save the Children's office, there were still many colleagues working despite the late hour, including her own daughter, Falsana. Sabina was a beautiful woman who, that evening, was draped in a graceful white and light blue *sari* with its six feet of cloth skillfully wrapped around her.

Sabina was forty-two when I met her but her story started when she was nineteen living in Dinajpur, nestled in the northwest corner of the country, where Bhutan and Nepal join India and Bangladesh. I settled in with a translator as Sabina told the beautiful story of the love she and her husband shared, their courtship and betrothal in Dinajpur, the rites surrounding their traditional wedding, the births of their three children, the dreams they shared during twenty-two years of marriage, and, finally, Adan's death and Sabina's determination to move forward, embracing life.

Sabina and Adan's life together began as an arrangement between two families, but Sabina told of the fairy tale twist that brought them together. "I was living in Dinajpur with my family and Adan was already living and working in Dhaka. His cousin lived next door to me and Adan asked if there was a nice girl that he could marry." Sabina smiled and said that her neighbor told her husband-to-be, "Yes, there is a nice girl next door and you can marry her." The nice girl was nineteen-year-old Sabina.

Soon after, Adan's mother came to meet her future daughter-in-law and liked her immediately – and, the feeling was mutual. This was a good thing. Often in traditional cultures, the mother-in-law serves as the "gatekeeper" and can wield inordinate amounts of power. In some traditional societies, a married woman must seek the permission of her mother-in-law for a number of important decisions, such as whether she can seek medical attention when complications arise in childbirth.

This was never the case between Sabina and Adan's mother. Theirs was, and still is, a loving relationship, much like the close bond that I share with Yvonne, my first mother-in-law. This friendship between Sabina and her mother-in-law has grown stronger since Adan's death – as has my relationship with Yvonne, representing an important link with my first husband's past.

Following the initial meeting of the families, the groom's father and Adan came to ask for Sabina's hand in marriage. She received an engagement ring during the visit, which was put on her finger by her future father-in-law. The first step had been taken toward joining Sabina's and Adan's families and the two young people in marriage. Once the families agreed to the marriage, Adan was then able to propose to Sabina, which he did in October 1975 in her family's home. He saw her, but Sabina did not look upon him. "How would I have seen him?" she asked. "In the culture at that time, I was too shy to look at him."

Sabina was married at her parents' house. I thought that this woman, seated in front of me, must have been stunning in her red and blue wedding *sari*. During the hours of celebration she remained seated. She wore two sets of jewels, one given to her from the groom's house and one from her own family. "It was so painful, it was all so heavy," Sabina admitted.

Not only were her jewelry and gown heavy, so was her heart. Sabina was young and was being taken away from the only life she had ever known with her parents and seven brothers – to live in an unknown city with a man she barely knew.

Throughout her wedding ceremony, Sabina kept her head down, even when a mirror was brought out, as is the custom, through which she was to see Adan for the first time. Had it not been for her tears, Sabina would have seen that Adan's face was kind and she would have heard him say, above her sobs, "Don't cry, I'll take you to your home tomorrow." They would share this home for twenty-two years and raise three children: two daughters and a son.

Their youngest daughter was only four years old when her father died of a heart attack. "My father didn't get proper treatment," Sharva often told her grandmother. She began to dream of becoming a doctor.

Adan died at home and his body was washed and put in a coffin. Ordinarily the deceased are wrapped in a clean white cloth and buried within twenty-four hours. However, Adan had chosen to be buried in Dinajpur, their home village. Sabina and her children made the long trek home with the body. This reminded me of the trip I also made to accompany Pascal's body from Canada to his final burial place.

In Bangladesh, the funeral and burial site are simple, unlike the extravagant, expensive tombs I saw in Haiti, which tended to bankrupt the poor, rural widows. Adan's body was removed from the coffin and buried in the traditional white cloth. As in all Muslim burials, the head must face Mecca. Sabina told me that following the burial, she did not wear jewelry, according to the custom. "I put my jewelry back on after forty days," she told me as she distractedly fingered her gold bracelet, "because I needed to feed my children." It's bad luck to feed children with a bare arm, devoid of any bangles.

Sabina chose to return to her home in Dhaka with her children after the burial, the city she first came to know as a scared nineteen-year-old. Since Adan's death, Sabina's life has changed dramatically. She now raises her children as a single, working parent in a city of six million people. As the evening descended on Dhaka and we heard the *muezzin* calling the city to prayer, Sabina told me that her relatives visit her often to ensure that she and the children are doing well.

Theirs is a close family. Her mother-in-law stays with her and the children when she comes to visit Dhaka, despite having two sons who live in the city. "She has stayed with me for the last four months," Sabina said of her mother-in-law's latest visit. "She still loves me very much. In me, my mother-in-law finds solace, she finds her son in my house." Much, I think, as my mother-in-law finds Pascal in my house.

Sabina also finds solace and reassuring memories in the house. "I see him in my dreams," she said with a faraway look in her eyes. "He looks very handsome, like when he was young." The day after a dream she offers a *Sadaqah*, a "giving of alms" by donating food to the poor or praying in the mosque. "As a Muslim, I do this when I dream of my husband," Sabina explained, as an act of thanks.

When Sabina thinks of her husband, she is reassured by her strong belief that he is in heaven. "I dream that he is in a flower garden eating fruit in heaven," she told me with a peaceful smile. Since her husband's death, Sabina's main goal is to ensure that her children are raised properly and to then join her husband. She added, "To be at peace."

Until she is reunited with her husband in the flower garden she sees in her dreams, Sabina looks to her children for comfort. Indeed, during our talk, Sabina's eldest daughter, Zainab, was never far from her mother's side. "All three children hug me at night and Acka, my son, adjusts the mosquito net over my bed for me," Sabina said. They have helped each other, as a family, to get through the difficult times.

Adan was obviously a good man, a loving father and husband, and is sorely missed. "I can't think of remarrying," Sabina continued, "after twenty-two years with my husband." However, she quickly added, perhaps for my benefit, "In our religion, you are allowed to remarry. My advice for a young widow would be to remarry if she feels very alone." This, I remember, was in great contrast to Rasika, the young Hindu widow some 150 kilometers away.

Although distance, religious customs, and beliefs may separate Rasika and Sabina, they shared a common pain and a common loss. They also shared the same aspirations for the future and the same values – to raise their children, to lead good lives, and to one day find peace. This is my hope for Rasika and Sabina.

My wish for Rasika has been partially granted. I was pleased to learn recently that she has managed, despite the staggering odds against her, to make a good life for herself and her five children. She continued to participate in Save the Children's programs and became an accomplished vegetable farmer. Through her involvement in different women's savings groups she managed to buy a cow and to grow crops and today works in her own fields as well as others to supplement her income. Her oldest daughter is now eighteen years old. Unfortunately, she was not able to complete her studies due to a lack of funding but her four younger siblings remain in school. Today, the youngest child, the one who squirmed on Rasika's lap during the interview, is ten years old and in the third grade.

A Good Pair of Shoes to Make Your Way

The High Lama explained to Conway, "And, most precious of all, you will have Time…"[17]

— James Hilton, Lost Horizon

During the summer of 1998, I reread *Lost Horizon*, the tale set deep in Shangri-La, immortalized by James Hilton. The first time I read the book as a teenager in upstate New York, the concept of "time" did not resonate as loudly as upon the second reading some eighteen years later. The second time unnerved me. There was an indescribable, almost palpable feeling that time was slipping through my fingers. Time was running out – but time for what? It preyed on my mind and the more I questioned, the more troubled I became.

I didn't mention this to Pascal. I thought that this feeling of time hanging heavily over me was a passing feeling, not realizing that the time slipping away was more urgent. Pascal and I were to have just two more months together. By September, our time had slipped away…

Three years later I found myself bound for Kathmandu and inevitably drawn to *Lost Horizon* and its enigmatic Shangri-La tucked deeply in the Himalayas. Upon arriving in Nepal my first reaction was that it should be Pascal, not me, in this mountainous kingdom. He had loved the mountains, believing they possessed a majesty found nowhere else on earth. Before we met, he had climbed Mont Blanc, Europe's highest mountain, and was an accomplished rock climber. I've always preferred the ocean but through Pascal's eyes and encouragement, I'd also come to appreciate and to respect mountains. We would spend clear evenings staring at the crown of Mont Blanc, its majestic profile white against the dark Alpine sky.

It would have been Pascal's dream to visit Nepal and to trek through its landscape; to pass by a base camp and to see the Buddhist prayer flags fluttering, the wind carrying their messages of blessings and hope. Upon my return from Nepal, I visited Pascal's grave and strung prayer flags so that they could catch the wind just right to carry prayers to him.

Being in Nepal was like looking through a kaleidoscope. There were so many colorful, disjointed pieces that turned and twisted before my eyes. There was so much to see and take in – enough, I thought, for an entire lifetime. As I began to unpeel layer after layer of mystery and understanding, I had to remind myself not to fall victim to the romanticized images of Nepal – not to ignore the fact that this mythically idyllic place was also stricken by great suffering.

The poverty was devastating and the civil war, which would last ten years and take some twelve thousand lives, was in its early stages. It was a difficult time during my stay and it wasn't always safe to travel too far outside the main district villages. I'd been sent to Nepal to write an anti-trafficking proposal to help children who were being cajoled, sold, or otherwise recruited for jobs, which would land them in brothels in India. Nuwakot was one of the centers of this horrendous practice.

On a sunny morning in late April, Shova, my friend and colleague, and I set off on our vertical path out of the Kathmandu Valley, and then headed both north and east toward Nuwakot District.

I'd asked Shova if she could arrange a meeting with some local widows during my visit. She told me that it might be difficult – but perhaps one or two would be available to speak with me. To her surprise and mine, twelve widows were waiting for me upon my arrival in this isolated town. The women had come from outlying villages and I wondered how the word of my request had spread so quickly. Some of the women had walked almost two hours and had voluntarily forgone a day's wage – a precious commodity in the life of a Nepalese widow.

The women represented a mix of castes and ethnic backgrounds. This was also surprising and still quite rare in this country, which officially declared the caste system illegal only some thirty years ago. This system, which dates back some three thousand years with its complicated interrelationships, lives on *de facto* in Nepal, especially in the outlying areas. The diverse mix of women who greeted me and their varying ages were immediately evident.

Dhanamaya caught my eye right away. (*The names in this chapter have been changed.*) She was a jolly, elderly lady who was wearing a type of turban on her head that she would wrap and unwrap during the interview almost as a stage actor would use a scarf as a prop. Despite the suffering and hardship she must have endured throughout her life, she quickly emerged as the group's entertainer, providing humor, a smile, and relief to her friends when they needed encouragement.

She was obviously well known by the women because of her outgoing, ebullient personality but also because of her role as the village midwife. Indeed, she most probably had helped many of women in the room give birth to their children over the past fifteen years. Pregnancy is one the most dangerous times of life for many women in Nepal. The lifetime maternal mortality risk is high – one in thirty-one[18] – and most births still take place at home with only the assistance of a midwife to help with delivery and any complications that may arise.

Seated close to Dhanamaya was Anita, a *dalit*, the name given to former untouchables. Anita's daughter was just five years old when her husband died. "Sometimes my youngest daughter asks about her father," Anita told the group. "My husband died in Kathmandu and she is still waiting for him to return with the biscuits that he promised her."

Anita wore a pretty flowered *sari*, which contrasted starkly with the story she told. The dress harkened back to a happier time when her husband was one of the top tailors in Nuwakot. "When my father accepted the marriage proposal, he was very impressed by my husband's tailoring skill," Anita told me. A bride at thirteen, she fondly recalled her years of marriage. "Sometimes we quarreled and sometimes we had fun."

There was more laughter than tears during those times for Anita and her three daughters when her husband was alive and providing for the family, before he died of tuberculosis. After her husband's death, his body was taken to the cremation pyre. The head mourner is the eldest son; the widow and other women do not accompany the body. A Hindu woman will often follow the cremation with thirteen days of *Kiriya basne,* or "sitting in mourning." It is a difficult time, considered a period of defilement, and characterized by a number of restrictions. Traditionally, the widow should not touch anyone during the beginning of this period. She sleeps on the ground and can eat only once a day. The food must be prepared by her alone and cannot contain salt or seasonings.

In the places I visited, the widows were seen as "bad omens" and were kept at a distance, often prevented from attending festivals and remarrying. Anita recalled the very difficult period after her husband's death and noted that the only time she received any sympathy was when she visited her *maiti*, or home village. In order to make her life easier, Anita converted to Christianity, and said, "It is far better for me."

All of the women in the group, except for Anita and Padma, were Hindu in this country, which was officially the only Hindu country in the world until it became a secular state in 2007. Padma is a Bhuddist and comes from the ethnic group of Sherpas, who have become famous for carrying heavy loads for trekkers hoping to conquer Mount Everest. It's believed that the Sherpa people migrated to Nepal from eastern Tibet over four hundred years ago. Indeed, Padma was different from the other women – both in her features and her demeanor.

When the women told me that they support each other and talked to other widows who were in a similar situation, Padma remained very silent. When asked, she very quietly added, "I do not talk to anyone about my problems." Suddenly the silent prayer flags fluttering in the breeze around the stupas of Kathmandu and of other remote Buddhist monasteries in Nepal came to mind. I thought of Padma and wondered if her thoughts were like those of the prayer flags – silent whispers in the wind.

Padma was dressed in a beautiful, deep purple *sari* and sat on her mat with her legs crossed behind her. While the other women had obviously come to the interview directly from hard and dusty labor, Padma was clean and tidy. She seemed financially better off than the others. Her shyness was almost painful to watch and I felt like an intruder into Padma's innermost world as I asked about her life. She hesitated, but once she opened up, her story and how she found herself amongst this group of widows in this lonely district of Nuwakot was intriguing.

Padma's marriage had been arranged, as is still the case for many marriages in South Asia. Her mother-in-law delivered the proposal to the guardians of then fifteen-year-old orphaned Padma. Without having met her suitor, she was wed. "I had seen him from quite a distance before we were married," she said. The couple moved to India but returned to Nepal to raise their two sons and daughter. Padma did not add many details about her husband or how he died, and with difficultly told us, "My husband was killed instantly when the logs he was transporting crushed him." Unlike many Buddhists, Padma told me that she does not believe in rebirth. "I have never seen it happen or heard of it happening. Once a person is gone, they are gone forever."

Her greatest challenge since the accidental death of her husband has been to raise her three children, who, when I spoke with her, were seventeen, fourteen, and eleven years old. She said, "There is no one to share this responsibility." Her in-laws, who still live in India, provide as much assistance as they can to their beloved daughter-in-law and grandchildren. "Without their assistance and that of my brothers," Padma quietly admitted, "I would not be able to manage." When we met, she was a shopkeeper in Nuwakot selling groceries – biscuits, sodas and sundries – to local townspeople.

Seated next to Padma was Satya who had been widowed for twenty-six years. Her husband fell ill from a fever and died. It sounded all too familiar – I had heard this tragic tale from so many women. Following his death, Satya was forced to sell her property for money to raise her daughters. Since then, she's worked, carrying bricks and sand, and worked in the fields – taking on hard labor to ensure her daughters' survival. Satya proudly mentioned that both her daughters, now in their early thirties, were happily married. But, admittedly, it had been a difficult journey.

These days, life is still not easy. "My daughters sometime come to see me," Satya said, but her loneliness was almost tangible in the heavy, still air of the room heated by the midday sun. Without realizing, we had lost electricity and the ceiling fans had been stilled while listening to her sad story. Despite the rising temperature in the room, Satya implored me to drink my tea, which had been placed on the mat in front of me. "It's getting cold," she said kindly as if to detract from her own grief. She had already finished her tea and carefully fingered her package of biscuits which she would save for later – a treat to be savored.

Satya continues to work in order to eke out what is a meager existence by any standards. While traveling in Nepal, what struck me was the sheer level of poverty. I'd visited many poor regions of the world before and had read all the statistics on Nepal – but had failed to fully comprehend the extent of the absolute poverty confronted by the people of this mountain nation. Satya brought me back to the reality of the situation. "No work; no food," she told me; it was as simple as that. "If I do not find work, I have to remain with an empty stomach."

The interview also confirmed something that I had already seen since my arrival – the jobs performed by widows are grueling. Widows in Nepal often perform menial work, such as carrying heavy loads on construction sites. It's common to see these women by the side of the road carrying stones and bags of sand suspended from a strap hung from their foreheads or carrying heavy bundles of harvested grains and vegetables atop their heads.

For Satya and the others, it has been a long, hard struggle – and they believe that it is their fate. "My husband was taken away from me by God," Satya noted as the women around the room nodded in agreement. "Once on the cremation pyre, he will not come back again."

Upon finishing, Satya asked about my experiences. When I told them about Pascal and my life since his death, the group, sitting in a large circle of which I was a part, very touchingly offered me condolences. Satya looked at me very sadly and said, "You look so young…" In the years following Pascal's death, I heard this many times. In fact, as was often the case, there were widows much younger than I in the room. In this particular case, there were many – including Bindra.

Bindra was married at age eleven. When I spoke with her, she was twenty-eight and had been a widow for six years. She is a Newar, the original people of the Kathmandu Valley. One of the traditional beliefs in Nepal is the sacredness of trees as the holy dwelling place of the gods – for the Newars, the most hallowed is the bel tree. Young Newar girls – between the ages of five and eleven – dress in traditional wedding robes and are symbolically married to the fruit of the bel tree during the elaborate *Ihi* ceremony. This ritual is meant to protect the girls if they become widows later in life. The women are never truly widowed because they are still "married" to the bel tree and therefore are not subjected to many of the degrading customs associated with widowhood.

Bindra was widowed when her husband died of tuberculosis. She is now raising a seventeen-year-old son – who is just twelve years her junior – a middle child who is fourteen and one daughter who is eleven, the same age as Bindra when she married. Both her father-in-law and mother-in-law died in quick succession after her husband, as did her brother-in-law. Bindra said that she has brothers but "they offered me no support." She has been left truly alone.

Midway through our session, two elderly women entered the room and walked quietly to mats placed off to the side. They explained apologetically that they had walked many miles to arrive in this small market village. They were close friends, which was obvious by the way each encouraged and supported the other as we listened to their difficult stories of hardship.

Sunita was the older at seventy. This was already quite an advanced age for a Nepalese woman, whose life expectancy is about fifty-seven years old. Nevertheless, Sunita was spry and alert and told us that she had walked over an hour to participate in the interview. She was wearing a mustard-colored sari that helped to hide the dust from her trek. Her sari and dark skin offset the gray of her hair, which was pulled back tightly in a bun at the nape of her neck.

Sunita told us that she was widowed nine years ago when her husband collapsed and died. "Probably from a heart attack," she explained. Her family included six children, only four of whom were still alive – two sons and two daughters. Sunita, a landowner, lived with her son, who is the traditional caregiver for elderly parents. After this brief explanation, she said little else but comforted her friend, Moya, as she spoke. Later, Moya said, "I consider Sunita like a mother."

Moya has appreciated this friendship through her ordeal, which began some nineteen years ago. Dressed in a purple sari, which overlaid a green-flowered shirt, she started by saying that she had four children. After her husband died, she took whatever jobs she could find, working up to fifteen hours a day to provide for her children. Her jobs came seasonally. "I worked in the rice paddy fields," she noted with a teary gleam in her dark brown eyes. For the hours she worked and the sacrifices she made, she was able to provide her family with only about fifteen rupiahs – about twenty-four cents – a day.

Moya had endured great suffering, including the disappearance of her daughter. "After my husband died, one of my daughters became mad and left," Moya said, "and I never saw her again." This was particularly distressing to hear. Since arriving in Nepal, I had been busy developing a proposal to prevent the trafficking of Nepalese girls and women from Nuwakot to Mumbai, India. I could not help but wonder whether Moya's daughter had become entangled with exploitative traffickers preying on the vulnerability of a widow's daughter. One can only hope that this was not the case.

The years had been difficult and Moya told us, holding back her tears, "My body is aching." When I met her, she was a peanut vendor, making barely enough to survive. "My son does not look after me. My neighbors help me though," Moya added with a grateful smile and a sideways glance at Sunita, her friend.

Moya brought home most poignantly that the life of a widow is neither good nor easy, which was foreshadowed some two millennia ago in the *Code of Manu*[19], one of the sacred books of Hinduism that forms a foundation for Hindu law, religion and social way of life. However, what also became evident was the resilience of the women and their drive to continue, despite their daily hardships, struggles, and loneliness.

There is a saying in Nepal, *Gatilo jutta layo, aphno baTo aphai banayo* – "Put on a pair of good shoes and make your own way."[20] These hard-working, resourceful women have done just that to make the best possible lives for themselves and their children. I thought of this the night before my departure as my friend and colleague, Shova, wrapped a white scarf around my neck – a traditional parting gift for safe travels.

Echoes Across the Sky

> *Finally to forget his sorrow, he decided to plant trees and flowers on the lands he had made... Then he took his wife's jewels and scattered them across the sky... Sometimes he calls out to her, his voice echoing across the sky much like thunder."*[21]
>
> – Filipino Folk Tale

I first visited the Philippines in December 1997. Pascal and I looked forward to my return home just before December 25 in order to make our annual visit to the south of France to visit his mother. I left with the security of knowing that Pascal would be waiting for me. I dreamt about the upcoming holidays as I made my long trip to the other side of the world. That Christmas was indeed a happy time. We visited friends and family – luckily not knowing that it would be the last Christmas that we would share together. My second trip to the Philippines came three years after Pascal's death.

The Philippines, which is over ninety percent Catholic, is one of only two predominately Catholic countries in Asia, the other being East Timor. Admittedly, I didn't look forward to returning to the Philippines. Despite it being beautifully decorated with more Christmas lights than I had ever seen, I also remembered Manila as a crowded and noisy city with pockets of extreme poverty. Reassuringly, I told myself to keep in mind the lovely people who make any trip to the country special. The second visit, I found a beautiful world unfold before my eyes – islands and blue sea, small villages and the warm, wonderful people – and again, the people's struggle against crippling poverty.

I met Rosaria in her small hamlet of Ungka on the island of Ilo Ilo in the western Visayas region. *(The names in this chapter have been changed.)* The Philippines is a land of islands – over seven thousand of them. Rosaria was in her fifties when I met her and was a mixture of what I would realize was very typical of the widows of the

Philippines: they were a blend of happy and sad – *masaya, malungkot* – and many of the interviews were punctuated by both laughter and tears, much like the Philippines itself.

The history of this island-nation is characterized by the same highs and lows. The people I met told me that their love of life and emotional tendencies were a legacy of the Spanish, who ruled the islands for some three hundred years after Magellan made landfall. It is also, perhaps, from the Spanish that the Filipinas have acquired their deep abiding faith and acceptance of their fate and their widowhood.

Rosaria began her story by telling me how she met her mother-in-law, a central figure – it seems – in any marriage, no matter the culture. She met Antonio's mother when she was in her early twenties, while working in the laundry room of a "rich man's home" in Ilo Ilo City. Her future mother-in-law thought that this lively, hard-working girl would make a good match for her carpenter son. When Antonio met Rosaria, he agreed.

There is a tradition in the Philippines that a suitor must win over the family of the girl he is to marry. In Antonio's case, he did odd jobs around Rosaria's house. She recalled that Antonio, who lived in a small village some thirty miles from her home, courted her in earnest. "Antonio would come to my house on the weekend and help fetch water and collect firewood. He courted me for a year. Suddenly, it came to my mind and heart that I was in love with him," she said with a shy smile, her eyes shining happily.

During the year before their wedding, Rosaria traveled with Antonio to his home village as well. She recalled that his relatives found her "not quite beautiful but attractive" and it was agreed that the wedding would take place after a five-month waiting period. This would allow time for preparations as well as for the guests to be informed and, most important, to raise the funds for the wedding celebration. Finally, after what Rosaria said, "seemed like an eternity," the couple was married in 1969, the twenty-four-year-olds eager to start their life together. Rosaria reminisced that she wore a beautiful white wedding dress and veil.

Following a short honeymoon, she and her husband lived with his family until their own house was built. One year later, their first child, a daughter, was born; two sons followed soon after. Their children formed part of what has come to be known as the "martial law babies" – the generation of children who were born in the years following Fernando Marcos's rise to power.

While this was a time of great upheaval and uncertainty in the history of the Philippines, life in the village continued as usual, and Rosaria and Antonio carried on with their lives, raising their children. All of this changed in 1976 when Antonio was injured in a carpentry accident. Rosaria told me that her husband suffered for a year and finally succumbed to his wounds. The children were still very young – the eldest daughter was six, the middle son was three, and the youngest son was just a newborn. Rosaria found herself a young mother and widow at thirty-one.

Much of what Rosaria told me about the first year of her widowhood sounded very familiar to me, having been brought up in a second-generation Italian-Catholic family. I knowingly nodded when Rosaria explained, "I wore black for more than one year," which was the case for many widows I met in the Philippines, as in many traditional Catholic societies. Younger women were more likely to shorten this period or to wear muted colors.

Although I didn't wear black exclusively after Pascal died, I remembered from my own experience what a difficult decision it had been to wear less somber, brighter colors – a symbolic re-entry into the world. One Filipina widow I met summed it up nicely. "After a year I could remove the black garments, but the feeling was still the same once I took off the black; it goes deeper than the dress."

In the Philippines, relatives gather on the one-year anniversary of a loved one's death to visit the grave and to commemorate the person's life. "I raised a pig and we ate it on the one-year anniversary as part of the gathering," Rosaria said. She also lights a candle each year on the second of November – All Soul's Day, the Catholic day of remembrance for loved ones who have passed away – and brings flowers to her husband's grave.

While there is no stigma attached to a widow remarrying in the Philippines, Rosaria told me that she never considered it. "No," she said emphatically, adding playfully, "but there were many who used to offer – I refused." Indeed, none of the nearly twenty widows I met was remarried, often citing the well-being of their children.

Life was difficult for Rosaria and her children after Antonio died. Yet she has accepted her husband's death and hardship as the "will of God," a sentiment that I would hear echoed again and again from widows in this very religious society. "I pray for my husband and have masses and novenas said when I have the money," Rosaria added. In Catholicism, novenas are traditional nine-day prayers; there is a special novena of mourning.

However, money remained scarce. "After my husband died," Rosaria said, "I was afraid not to be able to raise my three children." She told me that she took on many jobs in order to provide for her family. "I accepted laundry and ironing and also became a gambling facilitator for ten years," acting as a go-between for gamblers and the gambling lord. She also raised chickens, pigs and ducks.

As she recalled these difficult times, her eyes welled up with tears and she began to cry, wiping her face with a handkerchief. "My husband's family used to visit and volunteered to watch the children and bring them to school," she said between gasps, her voice cracking with emotion.

"My daughter, Regina, was an honor roll student and the teacher advised me to put her into extracurricular activities," Rosaria said, but added with regret, "I didn't have the money and had to refuse." Rosaria lost her daughter ten years ago when she died from complications related to asthma.

Brightening up a bit, Rosaria proudly noted that her eldest son received his degree in engineering and is now able to contribute to the family's income. He lives with her, as does the second son, who works in the local mall. She is proud of how far her family has come, recalling that her children often had to go to school without breakfast. "I was sad because if I had the money, I would have been able to provide better nutrition to my children," she said and added, "I was worried that they wouldn't be able to do well in school if they were hungry."

Rosaria has made the best of a difficult situation – having lost her husband at a very young age and then her daughter. Her two remaining children were doing well, thanks to the dedication of a hard-working and caring mother. She was still waiting to become a *lola*, grandmother, and this would come in time, she was sure. As for her husband, Rosaria knew that she would be reunited with him one day. "I expect we will someday see each other when I die," and added, smiling, "a long time from now."

Two days later I left the beautiful island of Ilo Ilo and returned to Manila. As the plane took off, I looked down on the island surrounded by the blue waters of the Sulu Sea. I thought that while life was difficult on Ilo Ilo for the women I'd met, at least their children had space to play and fresh air to breathe.

Masville, a squatter community in Metro Manila, could not have been more different. Its narrow streets, decrepit buildings, and polluted by-ways left little opportunity for children to run, to jump, or play; the children grew up in squalor.

Life is hard for the seven thousand families, some forty-two thousand people, crammed into this poor community. Six widows from surrounding squatter residences agreed to be interviewed in a building that served as the community room. The squalor of the streets was reflected in the building: the roof consisted of a patchwork of corrugated metal and wood. Hanging from one part of the semi-complete ceiling was a lopsided fan turning in an unsuccessful attempt to cool the room from the full heat of Manila's afternoon sun. There were earthquake safety signs plastered on the unfinished concrete wall and I wondered how well this quasi-building would hold up to the shocks of a tremor. Not very well, I suspected – and tried to put it out of my mind. Dead-center in the middle of the room stood the community's water pump.

To be seated there was indeed surreal. Yet, the children on these crowded, dirty streets somehow managed to enjoy some aspects of their childhood in their beautiful, unknowing and accepting way. Looking through a window with no glass, I could see the *sari-sari*, or small general store, directly across the street. I remembered thinking that it was a busy place. At that moment, as if in confirmation, I spotted a little girl peer up on tiptoes through the shop's window. She was full of excitement, trying to decide what sweet to choose. Finally, she reached for a swizzle stick full of sugar crystals.

The *sari-sari* remained in my line of vision until, unexpectedly, I spotted two little girls peeping through the window. Soon, as they gained more courage, they hung their tiny arms through the glassless frame and pulled themselves up to get a closer look. When they caught me looking at them they put their hands to their mouths to repress giggles and pointed in amazement. Perhaps it is not often that a foreigner visits this part of Manila. They were quickly shooed away when their laughter caught the attention of the group seated in front of me.

Once the women had gathered, I began the interview with the help of a translator. A few of the women spoke some English, so the conversation was a smattering of a little English and lots of Tagalog. To my surprise, the first woman to speak was Matilda, from Ilo Ilo. Matilda told the group that she was married at thirty-three and was widowed at sixty-eight. Her husband, Augusto, was a farmer; he had a wound that swelled and never healed, and eventually he died from the infection. Matilda's eldest daughter lived in Masville and after her husband died, the Ilo Ilo native also moved to the squatter community in order to take care of her granddaughter.

Matilda, who suffers from asthma, told me that she sees her husband at night in her dreams. "I can see my house, my husband, but he is not talking." Matilda wishes that he could speak so that she could have one last conversation with him. When I asked Matilda what she would say, she replied – looking at me but through me – "I would want to share the problems I'm encountering with him and ask him how to make life easier for our children."

Anna, also a grandmother, sat next to Matilda. She was widowed in 1987 following twenty years of marriage to her husband, Ernesto. He died of high blood pressure, which she attributes to the "demands of urban life" in the squatter community. Anna, like Matilda, also watched her grandchildren during the day and was also quite sickly. She suffered from diabetes and high blood pressure. Urged on by Matilda, Anna confided, "Even though I have lots of sickness, I want to live longer. I would ask my husband to help me to live longer. I can't give financial support to my children and grandchildren but I can act as a helper; a presence for them."

These grandmothers rendered a great service to their families. Many children in the squatter neighborhoods were left alone during the day, and many of them ended up as *tambay*, street urchins, or worse. This and the lack of education for these children were the worst fears harbored by the women after their husbands died. Anna remembered, "Aside from the pain, it was difficult to send my children to school. I didn't have enough money." After her husband died, this tiny lady became a street vendor, pushing her heavy vending cart through the crowded, narrow streets all day.

All of the women agreed that the first problem they confronted was the exorbitant price of the funeral, especially the coffin. I was told that the funeral can cost upwards of 25,000 pesos or some $550. Anna said that she did not have any savings for this expense and added, "My husband's death was very abrupt; I was not prepared."

Some of the women borrowed money; others were helped through the traditional *abulay*, money collected from their immediate family or community to pay for the expenses. Indeed, in poor rural settings or urban squatter communities, it is not uncommon for the family to go door-to-door to ask for money for the burial and funeral expenses. In such cases, I was told that it sometimes takes longer than a week to bury the family's dead. Delpina, a gray-haired lady who sat on the far right-hand side of the group, said that she had mortgaged her land in order to pay for her husband's funeral.

It was easy to tell that Delpina and Estella were good friends. They had a small rug-making business together and often shared whispers during the interview. Delpina's husband died five years ago from a heart attack. Estella had been a widow for three years following her husband's death from a cerebral hemorrhage. The ladies told me that their neighbors taught them how to make the rugs and now they have a sewing machine.

"The business would do better if we could get more remnants. We pay twelve pesos per kilo for the remnants but earn twenty-five pesos per kilo of carpet once they are made," the women say hugging each other in a spontaneous show of affection and courage in the face of hardship. The women were proud of their newly acquired skills and what had become a sustainable livelihood. However, Estella, some twenty years younger than Delpina with children to provide for, admitted this was barely enough.

Melinda also had young children – nine of them – ranging from six months to sixteen years old. She was young herself. She went to the cemetery every day to visit her husband's grave, despite her demanding schedule. Melinda explained that she sold preserved meats, such as hot dogs, on consignment but was worried – she often needed to spend her capital in order to pay for her children's school fees and for special school projects. Yet, she was adamant that they not miss out on their education.

Melinda had masses said on special days and planned a mass on her husband's death anniversary. It had not yet been a year since her husband was shot and killed during a violent confrontation in the squatter village. Some of the women in the group said that they had seen the ghost of her husband wandering the streets. They believed that he came to watch over his children. Luckily, all of the women lived close to Melinda and visited her as often as they could, "to keep up her spirits and to provide what comfort they can." Melinda was lucky to have such good friends to help her.

Melinda was in her early thirties and though the loss was very recent, I asked her about the possibility of remarriage. She firmly said no, fearing that a stepfather might sexually abuse her daughter – a harsh reality. Matilda agreed, shifting in her seat and stating, "Although painful, it is God's will. We have to accept the reality of life and think of the children… and keep the faith." On hearing this, Melinda seemed torn, hesitated and added hopefully, "I may be able to find someone like my husband, God may find me someone…"

But that was for later, once her children were grown. For now, her children were her first priority and, while she worried about them and their future a great deal, it was obvious that they also brought her great comfort and joy.

The strong devotion of all the women to their children was a common thread which wove its way through their lives along with their unwavering faith in the benevolent God found in Psalms 68:5, "…a father to the fatherless, a defender of widows."

Genoveva Erdoza Matute is recognized as one of the greatest Tagalog short fiction writers of her generation. In her *Story of "Well"* there is a beautiful passage – "Only those who know secret sorrows also know secret joys…"[22] I felt that this was true of Melinda and Rosaria and the other women I met in the Philippines. Each carried with her a secret sorrow but also secret joys – the struggle of surviving but also the satisfaction of knowing that they were providing for their children and working toward a better future for them.

How Many Tears?

Kitnay aañsoo teray sahraaoñ ko gulzaar karayñ?
How many sighs will soothe your heart—and
how many tears will make your deserts bloom?
   – Faiz Ahmed Faiz [23]

Only in existence for a little over sixty years, Pakistan's short history has been turbulent and troubled. When I arrived in October 2001, the country was again at a particularly difficult crossroads, an unstable foothold at the edge of the war being fought in Afghanistan. The country seemed to teeter precariously on the brink.

It was surreal to be at the epicenter of international turmoil. But, as is often the case when you are living it, danger does not seem as great as it does to the outside world. But great it was; I remember the many restrictions placed on my movements – even in the relative safety of Islamabad, the capital city. I was discouraged from leaving the city confines except for trips to the refugee camps where Save the Children implemented programs for Afghan refugees.

One such trip took me to Pakistan's North West Frontier Province or the "NWFP," home to the Khyber Pass and at that time, over a million Afghan refugees. As I traveled out of Haripur, one of the NWFP's main cities, the landscape transformed itself into beautiful rolling hills sprinkled with green brush. It was the time of year when the nomadic shepherds bring the goat herds down from the cold mountains to wait out the winter months. It's said that the hills are patient and will wait for the goats to return in springtime with its promise of rebirth.

The NWFP is an isolated land of ancient traditions and strong family bonds. As we made our way through the hills and villages, we quickly became lost, found our way, and were soon lost again. We stopped to ask villagers as they came from *Dhuhr* or midday prayers, for directions to the village where Hajira lived. *(The names in this chapter have been changed.)*

As we continued, goats scattered at our insistent honking and we passed groups of school girls in their blue uniforms. Women's heads were covered, as was mine, in this very conservative part of Pakistan. As we continued, there was time to tell stories and ask questions. I found out that our driver was a widower and it was obvious that he had loved his wife very much. "Friendship and marriage go side by side," he said as he navigated the country roads. Hajira, the widow I was to meet, had not been so lucky to have such a kind, loving husband.

Safa, a colleague and student of British literature, had kindly agreed to translate from the local dialect to English. As we approach a cluster of houses we encountered a young woman hidden behind her *dupata*, or traditional scarf, who pointed us to Hajira's village in the distance.

I met Hajira on an autumn day as winter preparations were in full swing at her sister-in-law's house. Later we found out that her own home, inherited from her husband, had no walls. Hajira and her in-laws welcomed me with open arms, literally. The Pakistani people are friendly and hospitable, and it gives you a warm feeling to be received into their homes.

As I entered the courtyard, Hajira stood before me. She was an older woman, but as is often the case, looked much older than her years. She told us that her marriage was arranged when she was seventeen or eighteen. As is still the case in much of the rural countryside of Pakistan, she was betrothed to her cousin. Hajira and Rafiq were married for about thirty-five years. She and her husband were poor – very poor. He was a laborer, paid daily, if he could find work.

Hajira mothered nine children, four of whom lived. Pakistan has a very high child mortality rate – one child in ten does not survive to celebrate his or her fifth birthday.[24] Hajira herself was lucky to survive the travail of nine births – giving birth is one of the riskiest actions a woman in the developing world will ever undertake. Many

Pakistani women still give birth at home with no trained midwife. There is a one-in-seventy-four lifetime risk of maternal death.[25]

Men and women do not often reach old age in Pakistan, as was the case with Hajira's husband. Rafiq fell sick and, while her brother-in-law helped out with medicines, Hajira said, "It was not a complete cure." She was not sure what caused her husband's death. "I think he died because of the pain in his belly," she explained. Her husband was wrapped and buried in simple white cloth, and, as is the tradition, she and other women were not present at the graveside during his burial. Hajira later visited Rafiq's grave, where she placed a stone to mark the burial site.

Following his death, Hajira observed the traditional *Iddah* period of mourning, which lasts for four months and ten days during which a widow traditionally does not leave the house. For the first thirty days of mourning, Hajira's family brought food to her due to the restrictions of cooking in a house of mourning.

Hajira said her first thoughts after Rafiq died were for her children. She worried, "How will I care for the children without their father?" Indeed, if Hajira and her family were poor before her husband died; now she was destitute. Even though there were no walls, she and her children inherited the family's house in line with the Islamic custom of *haq mahr*, much like a marriage agreement, in which a husband can decree what his wife will inherit after his death.

This is not always the case in other parts of the world. In some areas, the terrible custom of "property grabbing" or "widow chasing" is still practiced, in which a widow and her children are literally chased from their homes and their possessions are "grabbed" by others – usually the family of her deceased husband.

Indeed, widows hold a special place in the Islamic tradition and, according to the Koran, there is no stigma attached to widowhood. Khadijah, the Prophet Muhammad's first wife, was not just a keen businesswoman but also a widow when they met. They were married for twenty-five years until her death around 619, known as the Year of Sorrow – marking the year when both the Prophet's beloved wife, Khadijah, and uncle, Abu Talib, died.[26]

While there was no social stigma attached to widowhood for Hajira, she still struggled daily to provide a future for her children. Hajira told me that she had no regular source of income and was doing her best to keep her youngest son in school as well as her youngest daughter, Sara. While Sara was close to finishing, her son still had a number of years to go. The school fee was ten rupees per year – less than one dollar. Despite the hardship, Hajira confided, "I can manage this," adding, "he is my only son and I want him to be a good person, to have a good education, to be financially well-off."

Hajira sacrificed to buy secondhand books and used uniforms. Some of the villagers helped her with food and clothes for her children. She also hoped to earn money from raising chickens in the future. However, it is difficult for a widowed woman to borrow money at a reasonable interest rate and they often have to go to loan sharks who can charge up to 200 percent interest.

While Hajira would be able to ensure her children were educated, the prospects of a good marriage for her children were less than certain. Only one of Hajira's three daughters was married before her husband's death and she was clearly worried for the future of her youngest daughter, who was not yet engaged. Sara was in grade eight, but Hajira confided that she will need to find a match for her in the next year or two, "by grade ten." Hajira said, "I will face problems, because I will not be able to scrape together a good dowry."

The practice of the bride's family providing a dowry is a heavy burden in many societies. All the women in the room confirmed that it has become "fashionable" and they enthusiastically enumerated the items that would need to be included in the *kaikuli* as Hajira looked on nervously. "A double bed, dressing table, suitcase, and sofa," the women in turn shouted out, "a bindha, ring, and bracelet."

This type of dowry would be virtually impossible for Hajira to manage. Marrying her first two daughters had cleaned out the family coffers of all their valuables, especially the jewelry. "I had a ring, earrings, and two gold bangles that I sold to pay for the marriage of my first daughter, Nadia." Despite the dowry, Hajira told me with a sad look in her eyes, "Nadia's husband is not a good person, he beats her, they do not have children, and they are very poor."

One wonders what type of marriage Sara will be forced into without a proper dowry. If lucky, she will escape the fate that can be thrust on the daughters of poverty-stricken widows – arranged marriages to older men, sometimes three times the age of the young girls. Hajira is clearly worried.

Hajira's life has become more difficult not only financially, but also socially, since becoming a widow. "I am not discriminated against," she said, but later admitted that some people are not kind. "People look down on me. When I go to their homes, they hide their pots of grain. They are afraid that I will beg for food. Few people offer help because they know that I cannot repay them."

Luckily, this is not always the case. In Islam there is a tradition of *zakat*, a form of social welfare. Indeed, one of the many wonderful attributes that attracted me to my husband, Imran, was his kindness and willingness to help those in need. Long before we met, Imran was already helping the many widows in his village with a *zakat* on special Eid holidays. When Imran and I moved to America, the widows in his village came to his mother clearly worried and asked if Imran would still think of them now that he was living so far away. He does – every Eid he sends special *zakat* back to his village for the widows to buy flour and sugar for the celebration and to feed their families well beyond the holidays.

Even when Hajira's husband was alive, her life was not easy. This became evident toward the end of our conversation. When asked where she thought her husband had gone, she quietly laughed and shyly smiled and – after some prodding from the other women in the room – said, "Not to heaven. My husband was angry, not a kind man. He beat me repeatedly." Tears glistened in the corners of her eyes. "I pray that my children live long and spend a happy life, unlike me."

Hajira, like the mountains, has been patient, has never thought about remarrying and has concentrated on the welfare of her children and their future.

With the first true smile of the afternoon, Hajira told me that she would soon be a grandmother – a *nani* – and you could feel the joy in her voice. She looked at me and warmly added, "If you are still here, I will give you *gulab jaman*, the traditional Pakistani sweets in celebration." She could not hide her happiness. Today, this sounds very familiar to me.

When my daughter and son were born, my relatives in Pakistan handed out traditional *mithai* or sweets to their neighbors and friends in the village as a sign of joy and celebration. Today, Sophia speaks to her *dado* – the Punjabi word for paternal grandmother – on the phone, many miles from our home in Connecticut and you can hear the joy in her *dado's* voice when Sophia greets her with the traditional *assalaam-o-alaikum*. Most recently, even two-year-old Zachariah joyfully runs into the room when Imran phones home, joyfully calling for *dado* in the heart-warming way only a toddler can.

The most famous of Pakistan's poets, Muhammad Iqbal, wrote: *The world owes stability to mothers, their being is the repository of the possible.*[27] Hajira's hope for the future now rests with her children and grandchildren and she will continue to struggle to ensure that they have the best lives possible – good health, an education, and the possibility to break the heavy chains of poverty. *Inshalah*. God willing.

Don't Let Hope Slip

> *If someday you want to reach an oasis,*
> *Don't let the candle of hope slip from your palm.*
>   – Khalilullah Khalili[28]

For more than twenty years, Pakistan hosted the world's largest refugee population. There were between two and three million Afghans who took refuge in neighboring Pakistan from the time of the Soviet occupation beginning in 1979 through the fall of the Taliban in 2001.[29]

Ramena was an Afghan widow in exile in Pakistan when I met her shortly after September 11, 2001. *(The names in this chapter have been changed.)* It has been estimated that Ramena was one of some 30,000 to 50,000 women to be widowed in Kabul alone [30] or one of about two million women[31] to be widowed over the decades of violence in Afghanistan.

Indeed, it was striking to walk through the refugee villages in Pakistan or the streets of Kabul in Afghanistan and see how tragically easy it was to meet a widow, especially a young widow. It was even more tragically striking that each woman had a heart-wrenching story. The enormity of the loss experienced by the Afghan people is beyond comprehension. On a sunny October day, just days before Mazar-i-Sharif and Kabul fell to the Northern Alliance in 2001, Ramena told me her story.

Ramena's struggle began in 1993, three years before the Taliban's power spread to Kabul. At that time, she was a twenty-nine-year-old mother of five working in Kabul for an international humanitarian organization. By the turn of the new millennium, there were millions of landmines and unexploded ordnance in the country – and Kabul was one of the most heavily mined capital cities in the world. One day Ramena's world shattered. The years have not blunted the pain of this terrible event as Ramena told me of her husband's death. "My husband and Abdullah, my eldest son, were walking to work one day and they hit a mine." Abdullah survived; her husband did not.

Ramena worked hard to endure in Kabul after the accident, continuing to raise her children who were eight, seven, five, two and a four-month-old baby. Soon after being widowed, her brother-in-law demanded that Ramena marry him. "Widow inheritance" or levirate marriage is an ancient practice that can be traced to the Old Testament. In Deuteronomy it was decreed a widowed woman would marry her brother-in-law if she had no children. Although Ramena and her husband had children, her brother-in-law still insisted on marrying her and, as she told me, "When I refused, he had a very bad reaction. This led to problems concerning my property and also to fights with my in-laws."

Life as a widow was especially difficult for Ramena. Traditionally, after the death of a husband, most widows either live with their in-laws or return to their parents' home. However, Ramena's choices were extremely limited – she refused to be forced into the marriage with her brother-in-law and her parents were dead.

When the Taliban came to power, Ramena explained that the restrictions became even more repressive. "I especially had problems with the Taliban concerning my working." Ramena found herself alone, unable to work, and with five children to raise. With few options, Ramena joined the steady stream of refugees crossing the border into Pakistan near Peshawar. It was too dangerous for Ramena and her children to make the journey alone, so her brother accompanied the family to Haripur in Pakistan's NWFP and they officially became refugees.

Ramena was virtually alone in Haripur with no family close by that she could turn to. She had one brother who remained in Afghanistan and another who sought refuge in Quetta, also in Pakistan, but some 750 miles south from where she and her children settled. During our conversation, Ramena told me that her eldest son lived and worked in Peshawar where, she explained, "He makes special shoes" for victims of accidents, "and is able to help the family a little financially."

At first, life was very difficult in Pakistan, but when I spoke with her, Ramena was thirty-seven-years-old, had a full-time job, and was trying to make the best life that she could for herself and her children. "In Pakistan, I feel more powerful," she said. "In Afghanistan, I was very restricted."

Although Ramena still faced economic hardship, she was grateful for the chance to educate her children. Echoing the sentiments of many widows I have met throughout the world, Ramena noted, "I want a good education for my children." Her four youngest children were all in school and she made sure that there was enough money to pay the school fees for all of them – her sons and her daughters. Indeed, when education for girls and women was banned by the Taliban in 1996, the refugee villages in Pakistan became learning havens for future generations of Afghanistan's girls.

In the refugee village in Pakistan where Ramena made her home in exile, she was also able to ensure the basic health of her children. Ramena told me that with the money that she and her son earned, as well as some extra emergency funds contributed by work colleagues, Ramena was able to pay for a cataract operation for her daughter – an operation that would have been impossible in war-ravaged Afghanistan.

Remarriage is not prohibited in Muslim societies. Indeed, the Koran (2:234) states: *Such as you die and leave behind them wives, they shall wait, keeping themselves apart, four months and ten days.*[32] But, when I asked Ramena whether she would consider remarriage, Ramena swiftly touched her ears, then the ground and then her ears again – the customary movements for "God forbid" – and explained, "If Abdullah were not a good man then I could consider a second marriage, but I can't get remarried because my husband was so nice."

"The most important thing is education for both my daughters and my sons and good economic conditions for the children," Ramena said, adding with a smile, "and for me as well."

Her other hope was to one day visit Abdullah's grave in Kabul. Ramena said hopefully, "Maybe in the future I can return but now I can't because of the situation in Afghanistan. Always war." When I met Ramena, all she had were the memories of her beloved husband and their thirteen years of marriage, "I think of him all the time, he was a very nice man."

There was one more stop of the day – the Basomero Refugee Camp outside Haripur – where I met Badria. The Afghan refugee camps in Pakistan were different from the one I'd seen years earlier on the Mozambique border. It was not an endless sea of white tents stretched out along the horizon as far as the eye could see, but more of a village, established decades earlier as refugees began to stream across the border starting in 1978.

As we entered the camp, the winding streets led us down dead ends and a twisting maze of dirt roads and mud buildings. We were looking for a literacy class being held in a home where women gathered to learn to read. After many false starts, a child we met on the street showed us the way.

When I poked my head through the door, an amazing world opened up before my eyes. The courtyard was crowded with women of all ages, absorbed in their studies, sitting in a circle on hand-woven rugs and cushions that protected them from the earthen floor. As I looked on, a noisy hen running through the middle of their circle didn't warrant even a passing glance from the women who were hard at work.

However, visitors did not go unnoticed. I was warmly greeted and welcomed into the circle. Sweet tea with milk was handed to us in a confirmation of Afghans' tradition of *melmastia* or hospitality, which is shown to all visitors. I gratefully accepted the steamy, sugary drink and cakes and took my place in the circle. The literacy class continued and the women went back to their studies, listening to the volunteer teacher.

The class, sponsored by Save the Children, gave the women the chance of a lifetime – one that would not have been available to them in the Afghanistan they fled. In 1996, the Taliban banned girls from attending school and women from teaching. By the turn of the millennium, it was reported that 94 percent of all adult Afghan women were functionally illiterate. [33]

During the break, I was introduced to Badria. She wore a long sand-colored shawl that covered her head and draped down to her waist, overlaying a dark blue *shalwar kameez*. Her face and dark features seemed to blend in with the light brown woolen shawl. Badria looked old before her time – much older than her forty-eight years. I was sure that she had known great suffering in her life – which was confirmed when I sat down to speak with her.

Her story began two decades earlier when she, her husband, Zalmi, and their young children were living in Shewaki Village in Afghanistan. Her husband worked in a textile factory in Kabul and despite the civil war that engulfed the country, Badria remembered this as a happy time in her life – her husband had a regular salary and, as a government employee, also received rations of flour, oil, tea and soap. Badria's sister-in-law, who was part of the literacy circle gathered that afternoon, added that Zalmi was very kind. Badria and Zalmi had been married four years when he was killed.

Badria left Afghanistan over twenty years ago when she was in her mid-twenties. When her husband was killed, she was left to raise their three-year-old daughter and one-year-old son. After so many years, Badria re-visited the day when her husband was killed and the weeks and months that followed. She told us that Zalmi had gone to a neighboring village to visit a relative who was a *mujahidin* commander, fighting against the Soviet occupation which began in 1979. During the visit, Zalmi was caught in a major offensive. "Upon seeing the bombs falling, I fled with my children to the shelter of my father's village," Badria said, "I heard the roar of the rockets as they rained down on the neighboring village and was told that there had been a heavy loss of life." Badria remembered being desperately worried for her husband's safety.

This fear was well founded. Overcome by emotion, Badria told me that three days later she learned that Zalmi had been beaten by the Soviet soldiers with their Kalashnikovs and left to die in a pool of blood. He had been buried quickly during a lull in the fighting in his own clothes – not given the chance for a proper burial in white cloth or *kafan*. During the offensive, Badria not only lost her husband, but also eighteen of her close relatives – including cousins and brothers-in-laws. "I could not scream or cry; I had no tears," Badria remembers when she received the news. "I didn't know what was happening to me."

Today, over twenty years later, she still relives the trauma of Zalmi's death. Badria's teacher, who had been listening to the story while the other women prepared their lessons, looked at me and gently confirmed that while Badria is an excellent student, she has moments when her concentration falters. "Yesterday, when Badria was sitting for an exam, I noticed that she was having a difficult time," Badria's teacher told me. "When I asked her what the matter was, Badria said that she was remembering her husband and what had happened."

Badria nodded in agreement and continued to tell us of the hardships that followed Zalmi's death – she and her children were forced by her in-laws to resettle in Pakistan and to live with them in their compound. They had wanted her to remarry a relative – a type of "widow inheritance" practiced in many parts of the world. When Badria refused, she was repeatedly beaten and lost four teeth. When she speaks, you can indeed see that all of Badria's front teeth are missing.

In addition to the beatings, there was also the humiliation. As a widow, she was told that she should not try to make herself beautiful – her in-laws would not let her wash or change her clothes. "When I would sneak off in the middle of the night to wash, the next morning my in-laws would be very angry," Badria remembered.

Upon arriving in Pakistan, Badria was forced to carry mud and stone on her back to help to construct the compound for her husband's family. When the four rooms were finished for her in-laws, they did not help Badria build a room for herself and her children. Badria told me that the difficult life under her in-laws' influence continued for twelve years. "After twelve or thirteen years, an organization came and registered widows," Badria recalled gratefully. "They gave me money to improve my situation. She told me that she used this money to build a room in her in-laws' compound and was able to gain a bit more independence.

With the organization's help, Badria was also able to earn some money through making and selling handicrafts, such as *chadors*. "I was eager to work and to get out of grasp of my in-laws," she told me – but the grasp, though loosened – remained. When I met with Badria, she had managed to move away from her in-laws and settle in the Basomero Refugee Camp with her mother, her relatives and some 112,000 other refugees. Her life in the camp, while still difficult, improved considerably.

The years of suffering and deprivation had not curbed her desire to improve her life and strive for a better future – but had fueled it more. The spark had always been there. Even in war-ravaged Afghanistan, education had been a foremost concern. "I bought notebooks and pens for my children before fleeing to Pakistan," she told me, a far-away look in her eyes as she remembered the days after her husband's death. "I hoped that that they could start their education. Upon arriving in Pakistan, there were no schools established for the first two years. I registered my children for school as soon as I was able."

Her son, Zahid, went to school for two years in the village and was then sent to live in an orphanage for poor children; the orphanage also had a school. Badria, her pride swelling at her son's accomplishments, but shadowed with regret, told me, "Zahid received a good education from the school and was able to stay in the school until grade seven. He was very keen to continue his studies, but I couldn't provide for his continued education. He was forced to go to work to support the family."

Badria was also very insistent that her daughter, Lila, pursue her studies. For many years, this was a struggle. "My in-laws did not allow her to attend school." During those years Badria "home schooled" her on the Koran using her son's school books. This all changed when she finally escaped the deadening grip of her in-laws' family and relocated to Basomero. She and Lila enrolled in literacy and education classes run by Save the Children in the camp. Badria told me that Lila was married when she was eighteen years old. "I had to give Lila in marriage to a twenty-year-old carpenter in exchange for his sister to marry my son, Zahid," Badria explained, unable to afford the traditional dowry.

Badria hoped that her son, Zahid, would be able to continue his education. However, with regret, she told me that Zahid was not able to do so because of the family's financial situation and that he worked odd jobs wherever he could find them – such as making bricks or collecting plastic for re-sale. "My eyesight is failing because of cataracts," Badria told me, "Otherwise I could help him more by making and selling handicrafts."

Despite all this, Badria refused to give up hope of a better future for herself and her children. When I met her, she was just days away from graduating. Her teacher told me, "Badria is the brightest student in the class. She will receive materials and supplemental training to allow her to start up her own literacy classes." Glowing with pride, Badria added, "The last three years as a refugee in the new camp have not been wasted."

Badria's daughter-in-law was also studying in the courtyard that day. "I'm a better student than she," Badria joked. She motioned for Farhana and her beautiful grandson, Abdullah, to sit with her. Farhana told me that her mother-in-law is very kind. "Because she had a very bad life, she wants to give me all the love, care, and support that she can. She says if she is kind to her daughter-in-law then, in turn, there will be a place for her in her daughter-in-law's heart."

Badria dreams that her grandson will attend school and have a better life than the one she's led. She also dreams of returning to Afghanistan, "I will be the first to go, once I know that there will be peace and stability," Badria told me. She dreams of starting classes in her home village to bring education and hope to those who stayed behind.

I wonder if Ramena and Badria were able to return to their beloved Afghanistan to begin life anew.

Six years have now passed since I spoke with Ramena and Badria on that October day in the Afghan refugee camp in Pakistan. Many of the refugees have now returned home, eager to restart their lives that were so brutally interrupted. Even more years have passed since the husbands of Ramena and Badria were so violently killed in the decades-long conflict that engulfed Afghanistan.

There is a beautiful saying in Pashtu, "The stars are holes in the sky through which people in heaven look back on those who still love them."[34] I hope that the stars have looked down with kindness on Ramena and Badria. When the women gaze up at the startlingly bright points of light against a clear black-as-ink Afghan sky, it's my wish that they are reminded of the love they shared with their husbands and they are assured they are not alone on their journeys.

Part III: Forever Joined to the Sea and the Sky

They have been joined to the sea and the sky
May they rest in peace

Ils appartiennent maintenant au ciel et à la mer
Qu'ils reposent en paix

– Swissair Memorial, Whalesback,
Nova Scotia

August 2008

It seems the path of my life has often turned sharply when I least expected it. The autumn of 2001 brought one of those unexpected twists in my journey.

After the horrifying events of September 11, I moved to Pakistan. As unusual as it may sound, it didn't strike me as out of the ordinary. I've worked in the humanitarian field for most of my adult life and have visited many corners of the world. At nineteen, I began two decades of travel – first in Europe and later in Africa and Asia.

Somehow I was drawn to places such as Belfast during the "troubles" or East Berlin before the collapse of the wall; Johannesburg during apartheid or Malawi under Banda; so it came as no surprise to find myself in Pakistan in October 2001. I was sent there to work on programs for Afghan refugees. Little did I know that this assignment would begin a year of back and forth across the world, as I met, fell in love with, and married my husband, Imran.

It's now been ten years since I first heard the news of the terrible accident that took the life of Pascal and 228 others on board Swissair 111. After the accident, those trying to comfort me said that I was young and time would heal the sadness and grief. I didn't believe them but now I know that it took both time and grace.

Like Marilyn on the White Earth Reservation, my life has changed profoundly in the years since Pascal's death and I too find my life filled to overflowing.

Imran and I married in May 2002 in a traditional Pakistani wedding – a multi-day affair that included henna, gypsy dancers, and a feast for over one thousand guests – and settled into our new life in Islamabad. That January, we moved to the United States. I was already pregnant with my daughter, Sophia, when we left Pakistan and she was born in September of that year. Zachariah, our son, was born two years later.

I believe that I am able to fully grapple with these emotions and memories of Pascal and his death only now that I'm happily remarried with two beautiful children. Even then, the process has been both heart-wrenching and cathartic. It's still extremely difficult. But my life with Pascal and his tragic death are part of who I am – and I need to remember. It's only through confronting his loss that I'm fully able to move forward. I now allow my mind to wander back to snippets of a life long past – warm summer days in the south of France, walks around Lake Geneva, long drives through the French countryside.

After spending a good part of my twenties and early thirties living abroad, I finally set down roots in the United States. Today, I've given up my hectic globe-trotting and have settled into life in Connecticut. After two decades of traveling the world, I'm happy to stay put and know that I'm blessed to have a beautiful, loving family and a comfortable life – a second chance at happiness.

Many of the widows I met have not been as lucky; they have been constrained by cultural and religious customs and societal norms from truly moving on with their lives. Yet, as evidenced through their stories, their determination and hard work enabled them to bravely move forward, providing for their families and children despite the difficulties they encounter.

Pakistani Moon

On nights when the bright moon waxes in the clear sky, my children and I look for the "Pakistani moon" – a slight crescent astride a bright star. This beautiful moon in our Western Hemisphere reminds me of the two worlds my family embraces. It also reminds me of the many places I've traveled and the many women I've met – it's the same moon in the star-filled sky that Ramena looks up to from her home in the Afghan refugee camp and the same moon that Agnes surely saw on that fateful night in September 1998 from her small coastal village of Peggy's Cove.

Pascal's favorite poem was T.S. Eliot's "Little Gidding" and its timeless quote of self-discovery –

We shall not cease from exploration
And the end of all our exploring
Will be to arrive where we started
And know the place for the first time.[35]

During the years since Pascal's death, I've learned a tremendous amount from the widows I've met. Ten years ago, the burden of my loss was too heavy for me to bear and I reached out to these women to find out about their lives and losses and discovered a world of widows – much different from my own – one I never imagined existed. Their stories of deprivation and struggle touched me and much like in the T.S. Eliot poem, I finally arrived "where I started" and knew what I needed to do. I hope that through telling their stories, I can begin to give back to remarkable women such as the ones I met who, many years ago, gave me the strength and encouragement to heal.

The Journey Continues...

To learn more about the state of widows around the world or how you can help, you can consult the following resources:

WidowSpeak is a literary project and a humanitarian effort weaving a web of support around widows everywhere. www.widowspeak.org

Widows Rights International is a small UK based, nonprofit, non-governmental organization founded in 1996. It mobilizes action by working with international organizations, national governments and legal and other civil society organizations. www.widowsrights.org

For more information on Save the Children's programs, please visit: www.savethechildren.org.

Endnotes

[1] CNN. "Swissair Jet Vanishes from Radar near Nova Scotia: Unconfirmed Reports of Crash," 2 September 1998 (Posted at: 11:16 p.m. EDT (0316 GMT)), http://www.cnn.com/WORLD/americas/9809/02/swiss.crash.01/ (27 June 2008)

[2] T. S. Eliot, Four Quartets (New York: Harcourt Brace Company, 1971), 13.

[3] William deGarthe, *This is Peggy's Cove: Nova Scotia, Canada* (Halifax: Halcraft Printing, 1993).

[4] For more information on William deGarthe and his life, please consult: Douglas Pope, *DeGarthe: His Life, Marine Art and Sculpture* (Hantsport, Nova Scotia: Lancelot Press Limited, 1989), 68.

[5] Winona LaDuke, *Last Standing Woman* (Stillwater, MN: Voyageur Press, 1997), 75.

[6] Raymond Bial, *The Ojibwe* (New York: Benchmark Books, 2000), 13.

[7] For more information on the Indian Boarding School system, please consult: Julie Davis. "American Indian Boarding School Experiences: Recent Studies from Native Perspectives," *Organization of American Historians Magazine of History*, 15 (winter 2001). www.oah.org/pubs/magazine/deseg/davis.html (15 June 2008)

[8] Mary E. Frye, *Do Not Stand at my Grave and Weep* http://www.poemhunter.com/poem/do-not-stand-at-my-grave-and-weep/ (21 June 2008).

[9] Vance Vannote, *Women of White Earth* (Minneapolis: University of Minnesota Press, 1999), 126.

[10] For more information on Haiti and its history please consult: Jean F. Blashfield, *Haiti: Enchantment of the World* (New York: Children's Press, 2008).

[11] Diane Wolkstein, *The Magic Orange Tree and Other Haitian Folktales*. (New York: Alfred A. Knopf, 1978), 97.

[12] Rabindranath Tagore, *Gitanjali* (Dhaka: The University Press Limited, 1983), 10.

[13] Niaz Zaman, *Princess Kalabati and Other Tales* (Dhaka: The University Press Limited, 1994), 63.

[14] Statistics for Bangladesh can be found at: http://www.asianinfo.org/asianinfo/bangladesh/bangladesh.htm.

[15] Tagore, 102.

[16] Tony Halliday, ed., *Insight Guide: Pakistan*, 3rd ed. (Singapore: APA Publications, 2000), 62.

[17] James Hilton, *Lost Horizon* (New York: Pocket Books, a division of Simon & Schuster, 1960), 154, 178.

[18] Save the Children, *State of the World's Mothers 2008: Closing the Survival Gap for Children Under 5* (May 2008), Mothers' Index 2008.

[19] For more information on the law code of Manu, please consult: Patrick Olivelle, trans., *The Law Code of Manu* (Oxford: Oxford University Press, 2004).

[20] Kesar Lall, *Proverbs and Sayings from Nepal* (Kathmandu: Ratna Pustak Bhandar, 1994), 24.

[21] Liana Romulo, *Filipino Children's Favorite Stories* (Singapore: Periplus Editions, 2000), 36.

[22] Genoveva Edroza Matute, *None of the Bitter* (Philippines: University of Santo Tomas Publishing House, 1998), 81.

[23] Mahir Ali. "Tragedy and a Travesty," 1 January 2008, *Z Magazine*, <http://www.zmag.org/znet/viewArticle/16067> (1 January 2008). To read more Faiz Ahmed Faiz poetry, please consult: Faiz Ahmed Faiz, *The Rebel's Silhouette: Selected Poems* (Amherst: The University of Massachusetts Press, 1991).

[24] Save the Children, Mothers' Index 2008.

[25] Save the Children, Mothers' Index 2008.

[26] For more information on the life of the Prophet Muhammad, please consult: Muhammad Husayn Haykal, *The Life of Muhammad*

(North American Trust Publications, 1976).

[27] Mustansir Mir, ed/trans. *Tulip in the Desert: A Selection of Poetry of Muhammad Iqbal* (London: Hurst and Company, 2000), 151.

[28] Edward Girardet and Jonathan Walter. *Afghanistan*, 2nd ed. (Geneva: Crosslines Publications, 2004), 277.

[29] For a summary and timeline of refugees from Afghanistan, please consult: Girardet and Walter, 280-281.

[30] Girardet and Walter, 106.

[31] Sharmeen Obaid-Chinoy. "Forgotten Women Turn Kabul into Widows' Capital," *The Independent*, 17 May 2007, http://www.independent.co.uk/news/world/asia/forgotten-women-turn-kabul-into-widows-capital-449137.html.

[32] Muhammad Marmaduke Pickthall, trans. *The Glorious Qur'an* (New York: The Muslim World League, 1977).

[33] Girardet and Walter, 212.

[34] Suzanne Fisher Staples, *Under the Persimmon Tree* (New York: Farrar Straus Giroux, 2005), 221.

[35] T.S. Eliot, 59.

About the Author

Julie Mughal received her B.A. in political science from Syracuse University and her M.A. in International Relations from the Maxwell School of Citizenship and Public Affairs, also from Syracuse University. She has over 17 years of international experience, serving the past eight years at Save the Children, where she is currently the Associate Director for Development Communications. Prior to this, she served as the Asia Operations Manager for Save the Children, which included postings in the Connecticut Headquarters, Pakistan and Afghanistan. She spent nine years at the International Organization for Migration (IOM) in Geneva, Switzerland as a project designer and trainer, as well as a desk officer for the Africa region. She is currently on the Board of Advisors for the Susie Reizod Foundation and has served as the United Nations Representative for the non-profit organization Empowering Widows in Development (Widows Rights International). She is the author of a number of migration-related articles as well as articles related to the situation of widows in the developing world. She lives in Connecticut with her husband and two young children.

www.ingramcontent.com/pod-product-compliance
Lightning Source LLC
Chambersburg PA
CBHW051456290426
44109CB00016B/1785